KU-595-195

THE
CONCISE
WORLD
ATLAS

THE CONCISE WORLD ATLAS

OMEGA BOOKS *in association with Oxford Cartographers Ltd*

Published 1982 by Omega Books Ltd
1 West Street, Ware, Hertfordshire, England

Maps copyright © Oxford University Press 1982

Cartographic adaptation and revision by Oxford Cartographers Ltd
17 Beaumont Street, Oxford OX1 2NA, UK

Printed and bound in Hong Kong by South China Printing Company

ISBN 0 907853 25 0

All rights reserved. No part of this publication may be reproduced or
transmitted, in any form or by any means, without permission of the
publishers.

This book is sold subject to the condition that it shall not, by way of
trade or otherwise, be lent, re-sold, hired out, or otherwise circulated
without the publisher's prior consent in any form of binding or cover
other than that in which it is published and without a similar
condition including this condition being imposed on the subsequent
purchaser.

CONTENTS

Countries of the World — Population, Area and Land Use

COUNTRIES	POPULATION (to nearest thousand) a	DENSITY (per sq. mile) a÷b	AREA (in sq. miles) b	APPROX. LAND USE PERCENTAGES† Arable & orchard	Permanent meadow & pasture	Forest & woodland	Waste, city areas etc.
Afghanistan	17,480,000	70	250,000	13.7	4.9	2.3	79.1
Albania	2,075,000	189	11,000	17.4	25.4	43.7	13.5
Algeria	14,770,000	15.5	952,000	3.0	16.1	1.3	79.6
Andorra	19,000	100	190	n.a.	n.a.	n.a.	n.a.
Angola	5,430,000	11	481,000	0.7	23.3	34.6	41.4
Antilles (Neth.)	218,000	574	380	5.2	—	—	94.8
Argentina	23,983,000	22	1,080,000	7.0	42.6	25.2	25.2
Australia	12,296,000	4.4	2,975,000	4.0	58.1	4.6	33.3
Austria	7,371,000	230	32,400	20.6	39.1	37.0	3.3
Bahamas, The	195,000	44	4,404	1.1	n.a.	28.4	70.4
Bahrain	207,000	900	230	n.a.	n.a.	n.a.	n.a.
Bangladesh	75,000,000	1,360	55,000	60.5	9.3	15.0	17.1
Barbados	254,000	1,530	166	64.0	n.a.	n.a.	30.2
Belgium	9,646,000	1,804	12,000	30.7	23.6	19.7	26.0
Benin	2,640,000	58	45,000	16.5	4.0	34.8	32.0
Bermuda	67,000	3,190	21	—	—	—	100.0
Bhutan	1,100,000	60	18,500	8.5	4.1	60.8	44.1
Bolivia	5,060,000	12.2	415,000	10.3	13.6	25.8	18.5
Botswana	629,000	2.0	275,000	1.7	72.6	4.6	25.8
Brazil	92,238,000	28	3,286,000	3.5	12.6	60.8	23.1
Brunei	213,000	9.0	2,226	3.5	n.a.	66.8	15.2
Bulgaria	8,436,000	196	43,000	41.1	11.1	27.7	32.6
Burma	27,584,000	105	262,000	23.4	0.5	44.4	37.6
Burundi	3,475,000	315	11,000	37.3	22.6	2.7	35.2
Cameroun	5,680,000	31	183,000	30.2	6.9	44.4	49.3
Canada	21,854,000	5.7	3,851,809	4.2	2.1	44.4	49.3
Cape Verde Is.	272,000	174	1,560	9.4	4.2	0.2	78.5
Central African Republic	1,518,000	6.4	238,000	7.4	0.2	11.8	47.5
Chad	3,510,000	7.7	496,000	5.5	13.6	34.8	52.4
Chile	9,566,000	33	286,000	6.1	11.1	27.9	62.7
China	787,000,000	209	3,759,000	11.2	17.8	7.9	14.6
Colombia	21,720,000	50	439,000	4.4	17.8	45.7	54.9
Comoro Islands	270,000	320	838	36.9	8.1	—	30.0
Congo	960,000	6.6	132,000	1.8	13.8	16.1	33.2
Costa Rica	1,695,000	85	20,000	12.3	18.2	47.5	10.7
Cuba	8,250,000	188	44,000	17.2	34.0	26.1	22.7
Cyprus	630,000	175	3,600	46.7	10.0	18.5	24.8
Czechoslovakia	14,418,000	292	49,000	42.5	13.9	34.8	9.2
Denmark	4,910,000	288	17,000	62.9	7.5	9.3	20.3
Djibouti	125,000	14	8,900	1.1	11.1	0.4	88.5
Dominican Republic	4,174,000	222	106,000	21.9	17.8	45.7	14.6
Ecuador	6,300,000	59	106,000	10.7	8.1	54.9	26.3
Egypt	34,130,000	88	386,000	2.6	n.a.	—	97.3
El Salvador	3,390,000	414	8,200	30.3	28.2	23.7	17.8
Equatorial Guinea	286,000	26	11,000	3.7	3.7	81.6	10.7
Ethiopia	24,769,000	65	395,000	10.3	56.4	6.8	26.0
Fiji	519,000	74	7,000	16.4	44.0	38.5	1.1
Finland	4,703,000	36	130,000	8.1	0.4	64.6	26.9
France	51,260,000	241	213,000	38.1	24.3	24.1	15.8
Gabon	485,000	4.7	103,000	0.5	18.3	74.7	6.5
Gambia, The	375,000	93	4,000	17.7	35.4	14.7	43.9
Germany, F.D.R.	61,682,000	643	96,000	33.4	23.5	29.0	14.1
Germany, G.D.R.	17,097,000	407	42,000	46.2	13.3	27.8	13.3
Ghana	8,600,000	93	92,000	10.7	1.0	29.0	13.3
Greece	8,835,000	173	51,000	29.2	30.0	10.3	12.1
Greenland (Dan.)	47,000	—	840,000	—	—	—	100.0
Guadeloupe (Dan.)	323,000	468	690	29.2	9.0	32.6	29.2
Guatemala	5,350,000	127	42,000	13.5	5.3	44.4	36.8
Guiana, French	44,000	1.3	35,000	—	0.6	95.0	4.4
Guinea	4,010,000	42	95,000	7.3	11.8	6.3	n.a.
Guinea Bissau	530,000	37	14,000	7.3	11.8	6.3	n.a.
Guyana	742,000	8.9	83,000	0.7	84.3	25.2	43.4
Haiti	4,768,000	476	11,000	13.4	18.0	3.9	43.4
Honduras	2,495,000	58	43,000	7.3	30.5	25.2	35.3
Hong Kong (Br.)	4,050,000	10,125	400	12.6	1.4	45.8	52.1
Hungary	10,295,000	296	36,000	60.7	12.6	9.7	17.0
Iceland	203,000	5.0	40,000	0.7	22.1	—	77.9
India	550,370,000	436	1,263,000	49.6	4.3	17.1	29.0
Indonesia	124,890,000	170	736,000	16.2	7.0	63.8	26.9
Iran	29,780,000	47	628,000	16.7	9.5	7.3	81.6
Ireland (Republic)	2,921,000	108	27,000	18.0	49.0	2.8	30.2
Israel	3,010,000	376	8,000	19.9	33.9	4.6	41.6
Italy	54,080,000	466	116,000	50.8	17.1	20.2	11.9
Ivory Coast	4,195,000	33	124,000	6.4	—	44.4	36.3
Jamaica	1,959,000	445	4,400	21.1	23.4	19.2	25.8
Japan	104,660,000	732	143,000	16.2	2.6	68.7	12.5
Jordan	2,160,000	58	37,000	11.6	2.2	0.7	85.5
Kampuchea	6,701,000	96	70,000	16.2	2.6	73.9	23.1
Kenya	11,690,000	53	220,000	2.9	6.7	2.9	85.5
Kiribati	58,000	220	264	15.7	n.a.	n.a.	n.a.
Korea, North	14,280,000	304	47,000	22.9	0.2	74.4	9.8
Korea, South	32,430,000	853	38,000	22.9	0.2	67.1	9.8
Kuwait	990,000	143	5,800	—	3.4	—	33.9
Laos	3,030,000	33	90,000	3.4	1.0	59.3	61.4
Lebanon	2,645,000	780	3,400	28.5	9.1	13.0	32.0
Leeward Is.	160,000	385	418	43.0	11.7	13.0	32.0
Lesotho	1,040,000	87	12,000	11.7	82.2	0.1	82.1
Liberia	1,150,000	27	43,000	34.5	8.0	32.5	30.8
Libya	2,010,000	3	679,000	2.2	8.0	0.2	89.9
Liechtenstein	21,000	334	62	26.7	24.7	25.0	18.8
Luxembourg	337,000	337	1,000	26.7	24.7	25.0	18.8
Madagascar	6,643,000	29	230,000	4.9	43.7	21.7	21.4
Malawi	4,398,000	119	37,000	24.7	52.0	24.7	53.1
Malaysia	10,583,000	82	128,000	18.9	65.7	18.9	15.6
Maldive Islands	115,000	1,000	115	1	n.a.	3.8	28.6
Mali	5,140,000	11	465,000	50.0	n.a.	n.a.	50.0
Malta	323,000	2,608	121	50.0	n.a.	n.a.	50.0
Martinique (Fr.)	332,000	795	420	29.1	18.2	24.5	28.2
Mauritania	1,140,000	3	419,000	0.2	36.2	13.9	11.8
Mauritius	823,000	1,160	720	50.6	16.1	21.5	25.7
Mexico	50,830,000	67	760,000	12.5	40.1	22.1	20.6
Mongolia	1,240,000	2.0	604,000	2.3	16.3	10.0	2.0
Morocco	15,050,000	88	171,000	17.2	12.0	12.0	53.1
Mozambique	8,233,000	28	298,000	3.4	56.2	24.8	28.6
Namibia	615,000	1.9	318,000	6.4	64.2	32.2	40.6
Nepal	10,845,000	200	54,000	13.0	14.2	32.2	24.3
Netherlands	13,190,000	1,015	13,000	28.8	38.3	8.6	24.3
New Caledonia (Fr.)	100,600	13.7	7,330	4.3	21.4	14.5	59.8
New Zealand	2,850,000	27	104,000	1.8	47.8	23.2	26.0
Nicaragua	1,915,000	34	57,000	6.6	6.6	46.2	41.1
Niger	4,130,000	9	459,000	2.3	11.8	2.3	73.6
Nigeria	63,870,000	179	357,000	23.6	12.0	34.2	n.a.
Norway	3,851,000	32	125,000	2.6	0.5	27.1	75.2
Oman	680,000	8.3	82,000	n.a.	n.a.	n.a.	n.a.
Pakistan	58,500,000	160	366,000	27.5	n.a.	3.8	n.a.
Panama	1,417,000	49	29,000	7.5	11.0	80.5	1.0
Papua New Guinea	2,315,000	12.5	184,000	2.2	24.3	n.a.	22.5
Paraguay	2,303,000	14.6	157,000	2.0	21.7	51.0	14.6
Philippines	14,010,000	28	496,000	26.4	11.0	41.2	21.4
Poland	32,555,000	274	120,000	50.3	13.7	25.8	10.2
Portugal	9,560,000	273	35,000	49.2	6.0	25.8	16.7
Puerto Rico (U.S.)	2,754,000	800	3,400	30.4	35.3	13.3	21.0
Qatar	445,000	459	970	24.7	8.0	38.2	29.1
Reunion (Fr.)	445,000	459	970	44.1	18.2	26.8	10.9
Romania	20,101,000	218	92,000	37.8	33.0	5.9	23.3
Rwanda	3,500,000	350	10,000	31.3	37.7	0.8	61.3
San Marino	19,000	791	24	0.2	—	—	—
São Tomé and Principe	66,000	186	372	28.0	—	27.1	44.5
Sa'udi Arabia	7,200,000	7.8	927,000	0.2	37.7	0.8	61.3
Senegal	3,780,000	49	76,000	28.0	1.0	27.1	44.5
Seychelles	51,000	318	160	42.1	—	14.0	44.5
Sierra Leone	2,512,000	87	28,000	51.1	30.7	14.0	56.9
Singapore	2,017,000	9,000	244	5.0	—	20.7	56.9
Solomon Islands	215,000	18.6	11,500	1.5	n.a.	22.6	43.6
Somali Republic	2,730,000	45	246,000	9.9	32.3	23.0	14.8
South Africa	21,282,000	45	472,000	9.9	74.0	23.0	8.1
Spain	34,130,000	175	195,000	40.8	28.1	50.7	20.5
Sri Lanka	12,240,000	490	25,000	28.6	0.2	50.7	51.1
Sudan	15,186,000	15	967,000	2.6	9.6	45.0	51.1
Surinam (Neth.)	410,000	61	6,700	0.3	—	45.0	19.9
Swaziland	410,000	47	6,700	7.1	73.4	7.4	4.7
Sweden	8,110,000	47	173,260	7.1	1.2	50.0	41.7
Switzerland	6,230,000	389	16,000	6.9	42.2	23.8	23.7
Syria	6,450,000	90	72,000	36.9	33.0	2.4	28.7
Taiwan	14,350,000	1,025	14,000	24.7	0.2	70.9	32.5
Tanzania	13,630,000	15	364,000	12.7	36.9	37.6	12.2
Thailand	34,738,000	175	198,000	21.9	1.2	52.8	20.6
Togo	1,815,000	86	21,000	38.2	3.5	45.0	10.7
Tonga	90,000	333	270	66.9	—	12.4	10.7
Trinidad and Tobago	1,040,000	515	1,980	34.1	2.0	45.0	19.9
Tunisia	5,027,000	79	63,362	34.6	45.2	6.7	13.5
Turkey	36,160,000	122	296,000	33.5	36.2	13.5	16.8
Uganda	10,130,000	111	91,000	16.0	—	7.0	n.a.
Union of Soviet Socialist Republics	242,000,000	28	8,648,000	10.3	16.6	40.6	32.5
United Arab Emirates	135,000	4.2	32,000	—	n.a.	13.9	n.a.
United Kingdom	55,534,000	588	94,500	30.7	49.7	7.4	12.2
United States of America	207,010,000	58	3,554,000	20.2	27.4	42.2	20.6
Upper Volta	5,278,000	49	106,000	17.9	37.2	49.1	10.7
Uruguay	2,862,000	37	72,000	12.0	74.1	3.2	10.7
Vanuatu	112,000	19.6	5,700	5.7	18.3	52.6	23.4
Venezuela	10,035,000	28	352,000	29.9	7.5	82.6	60.0
Viet-Nam	39,672,000	308	129,000	33.9	3.0	36.2	26.9
Western Sahara	63,000	—	105,000	—	—	—	n.a.
Windward Is.	384,000	464	828	6.9	31.3	36.2	20.6
Yemen A.R.	5,900,000	79	75,000	32.5	25.2	6.8	58.9
Yemen, P.D.R.	1,220,000	10.9	112,000	0.9	34.4	7.9	n.a.
Yugoslavia	20,500,000	207	99,000	32.5	25.2	34.4	7.9
Zaire	22,480,000	25	906,000	20.9	1.0	42.7	35.4
Zambia	4,208,000	14	290,000	2.0	43.8	60.0	3.6
Zimbabwe	5,090,000	33	150,000	4.7	12.5	60.0	22.8

— None   n.a. Not Available   For further information see The Oxford Economic Atlas of the World.   † Percentages are calculated from figures given in FAO Year-Book. They do not necessarily total 100 per cent.   Water is included as waste land.

World : Political

© Oxford University Press

Scale 1:165 000 000

Modified Gall Projection

Abbreviations (legend):

- Alb. Albania
- Aust. Austria
- Belg. Belgium
- Bh. Bhutan
- Ber. Brunei
- Ca. Cameroun
- Cen. Af. Rep. Central African Republic
- Cyp. Cyprus
- Czech. Czechoslovakia
- Dom. Rep. Dominican Republic
- E. Ger. East Germany
- Eq. Gui. Equatorial Guinea
- Gui. Guinea
- Hun. Hungary
- Isr. Israel
- Jor. Jordan
- Kam. Kampuchea
- Leb. Lebanon
- Lux. Luxembourg
- Mal. Malawi
- N.C. New Caledonia
- Neth. Netherlands
- Q. Qatar
- R. Rwanda
- S. Singapore
- S.L. Sierra Leone
- Sur. Surinam
- Sw. Switzerland
- T. Togo
- Thai. Thailand
- U. A. E. United Arab Emirates
- U. K. United Kingdom
- W. Ger. West Germany
- Y. Yemen
- Yemen P. D. R. Yemen Peoples Democratic Republic
- Yugo. Yugoslavia
- Zim. Zimbabwe

Map labels:

Date Line · 60°N · 30°N · Tropic of Cancer · Equator · 30°S · New Zealand

Japan · N.Korea · S.Korea · Taiwan · Hong Kong · Philippines · Papua New Guinea · N.C. · Australia

Union of Soviet Socialist Republics · Mongolia · China · Indonesia · Malaysia · Vietnam · Kam. · Thai. · Bur. · Bangladesh · Nepal · Bh. · India · Sri Lanka · Pakistan · Afghanistan · Iran · U.A.E. · Oman · Kuwait · Saudi Arabia · Yemen · Yemen P. D. R. · Djibouti · Somali Rep. · Seychelles · Mauritius · Réunion (Fr.) · Madagascar

180° · 150°E · 120°E · 90°E · 60°E

Iraq · Turkey · Syria · Leb. · Isr. · Jor. · Cyp. · Greece · Bulgaria · Romania · Yugo. · Hun. · Aust. · Italy · Malta · Tunisia · Ethiopia · Sudan · Egypt · Libya · Chad · Niger · Uganda · Kenya · Zaire · Congo · Gabon · Cen. Af. Rep. · Cabinda · Angola · Zambia · Tanzania · Burundi · R. · Malawi · Mozambique · Zimbabwe · Botswana · Namibia (S. W. Africa) · Rep. of South Africa · Swaziland · Lesotho

Sweden · Finland · Norway · Denmark · Neth. · E.Ger. · W. Ger. · Poland · Czech. · Belg. · Lux. · France · Spain · Portugal · Gibraltar · Ireland · U. K. · Morocco · Algeria · Mali Rep. · Mauritania · Western Sahara · Senegal · Gambia · Guinea Bissau · Gui. · S. L. · Liberia · Ivory Coast · Upper Volta · Ghana · Togo · Benin · Nigeria · Eq. Gui. · Canary Is.(Sp.) · Cape Verde Is.

Arctic Circle · Iceland · Greenland · Azores · Bermuda · 0° · 30°E

Canada · United States of America · Mexico · Bahamas · Cuba · Haiti · Dom.Rep. · Jamaica · Belize · Guatemala · El Salvador · Honduras · Nicaragua · Costa Rica · Panama · Trinidad and Tobago · Venezuela · Colombia · Ecuador · Galapagos Is. (Ec.) · Peru · Brazil · Bolivia · Paraguay · Uruguay · Chile · Argentina · Falkland Is. (U.K.) · Guyana · Sur. · French Guiana

Alaska (U.S.A.) · Hawaii (U.S.A.) · Tropic of Cancer · Equator · Tropic of Capricorn · Antarctic Circle

60°N · 30°N · 30°S · 60°S · 180° · 150°W · 30°W · Date Line

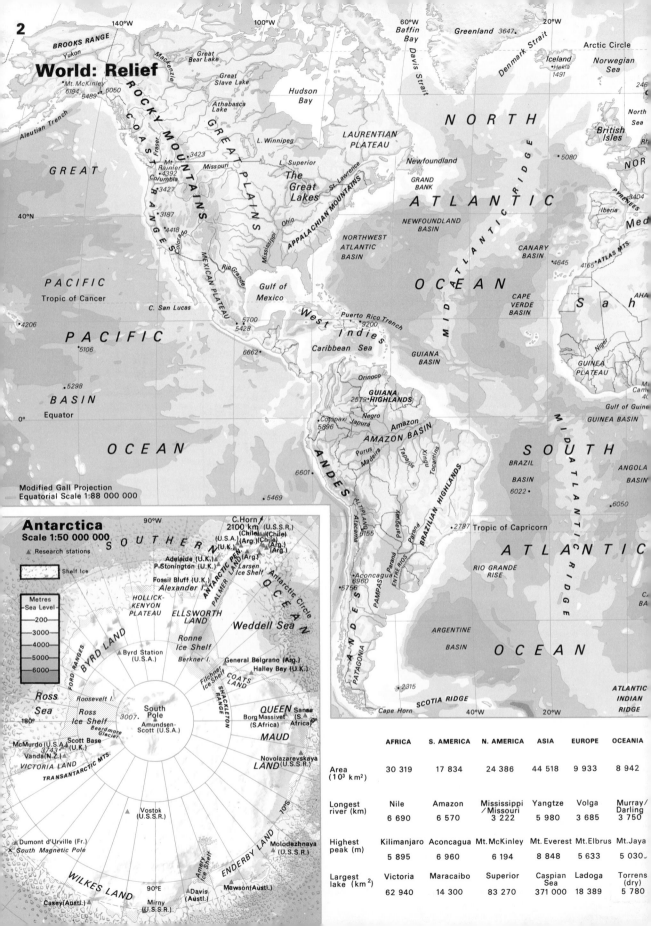

World: Relief

Modified Gall Projection
Equatorial Scale 1:88 000 000

Antarctica
Scale 1:50 000 000

▲ Research stations

Shelf Ice

Metres
Sea Level
- 200
- 3000
- 4000
- 5000
- 6000

	AFRICA	S. AMERICA	N. AMERICA	ASIA	EUROPE	OCEANIA
Area (10³ km²)	30 319	17 834	24 386	44 518	9 933	8 942
Longest river (km)	Nile 6 690	Amazon 6 570	Mississippi /Missouri 3 222	Yangtze 5 980	Volga 3 685	Murray/ Darling 3 750
Highest peak (m)	Kilimanjaro 5 895	Aconcagua 6 960	Mt.McKinley 6 194	Mt.Everest 8 848	Mt.Elbrus 5 633	Mt.Jaya 5 030
Largest lake (km²)	Victoria 62 940	Maracaibo 14 300	Superior 83 270	Caspian Sea 371 000	Ladoga 18 389	Torrens (dry) 5 780

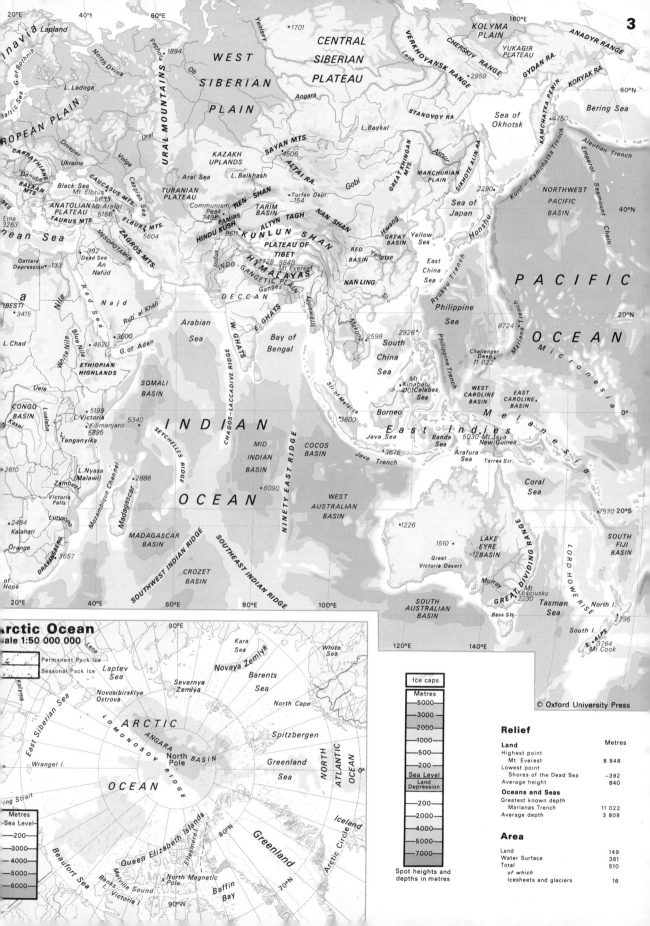

4

U.S.S.R.

International Date Line
Bering Strait (USSR) (US)

Bering Sea

St. Matthew I. (US)

Nunivak

Cape Newenham

Bristol Bay

Alaska Peninsula

Aleutian Range

PACIFIC OCEAN

Nome
Norton Sound

Bethel

Kuskokwim

Iliamna

Kodiak I.

Cape Lisburne

Point Barrow

Kotzebue

Seward Peninsula

St. Lawrence I. (US)

Diomede Is. (USSR) (US)

114b.

Brooks Range

MT. DOONERAK 2299

2816

A L A S K A

Yukon

Galena

McGrath

Farewell

Anchorage

Cordova

Valdez

Seward

Kenai Peninsula

Montague I.

Chichagof I.

Juneau

Prince of Wales I.

Ketchikan

Queen Charlotte Is.

Prince Rupert

Kitimat

Skeena

Queen Charlotte Sound

MT. WADDINGTON 4042

Vancouver I. 2200

Port Alberni

Vancouver

Victoria

Bellingham

Seattle

Tacoma

MT. RAINIER 4392

Portland

Oregon City

MT. HOOD 3427

Columbia

Eureka

Cape Mendocino

LASSEN PEAK 3186

MT. SHASTA 3317

Klamath Falls

Coast Ranges

Cascade

Willamette

Sacramento

Carson City

Sacramento

Tanana

Nenana

Fairbanks

Fort Yukon

MT. McKINLEY 6187

Willow

South

Summit

Kennicott

ALASKA

Alaska Range

MT. LOGAN 6050

MT. ST. ELIAS 5489

VANCOUVER

St. Elias Mts.

Skagway

YUKON

Alaskan Highway

Whitehorse

ROCKY MOUNTAINS

Coast Mountains

BRITISH COLUMBIA

Dawson

2499

Mackenzie Mountains

2758

2470

Demarcation Pt.

Aklavik

Fort McPherson

Arctic Circle

Fort Mackenzie

Liard

Fort Nelson

2786

Dawson Creek

PINE PASS

Prince George

Fraser

MT. ROBSON 3954

YELLOWHEAD PASS

KICKING HORSE PASS 3618

Banff

Bow

Kamloops

Kelowna

Penticton

Columbia

1360

CROWSNEST PASS

Columbia

Kootenay

Spokane

Snake

Blue Mts.

La Grande

Boise

Bitterroot Range

Salmon River Mts.

3858

Snake

Idaho Falls

Pocatello 4202

Great Salt Lake

Ogden

Salt Lake City

ARCTIC OCEAN

Queen Elizabeth

Borden I. Sver

Prince Patrick I.

McClure Str.

Parry Is.

Melville I.

Ma

Viscount Melville Sd.

Banks Island

Victoria Island

Cambridge Bay ·206

126°

Lake Garry

Dubawn

Kas Lak

M'Clintock

Beaufort Sea

Limit of pack ice average min. (autumn)

Cape Dalhousie

Herschel I.

Tuktoyaktuk

Inuvik

Mackenzie

Cape Bathurst

Cape Parry

Colville L.

Norman Wells

Great Bear Lake

Coppermine 610

Coronation Gulf

N O R T H W E S T

Rae

Yellowknife

Fort Simpson

Fort Providence

Great Slave Lake

Fort Resolution

Ft. Smith

Uranium City

Pine Pt.

Nonacho Lake

L. Athabasca

Fort McMurray

Mackenzie

Peace

Kas Lak

Wollaston L.

Rein Lake

Lynn Lake

Dubawn Lake

Nonacho Lake

ALBERTA

Ft. St. John

Peace River

Grande Prairie

Athabasca

Edmonton

Red Deer

Calgary

Medicine Hat

Lethbridge

Swift Current

Havre

Great Falls

Helena

Butte

Missouri

Yellowstone

3917

LARAMIE PEAK 3132

N. Platte

Bismarck

Abe

1045

2155

4013

Powd

Green River

Cheyenne

105°W

100°W

SASKATCHEWAN

Flin Flon M

Prince Albert

North Battleford

Saskatoon

Saskatchewan The Pas

L. Winnipegosis

Moose Jaw

Regina

Yorkton

Brando

792

823

796

U N I T E D   S T A T E S

C A N A D A

COLUMBIA MOUNTAINS

© Oxford University Press
Zenithal Equidistant Projection 130°W

Canada

Scale 1:19 000 000

0   200   400   600 km

Metres
5000
3000
2000
1000
500
300
200
100
Sea level
Land
depression
Spot heights
in metres

Boundaries International (in sea) (disputed)
Internal

Highways
Railways
Airports   International ⊕ Domestic ○
Canals   Seasonal
                           rivers, lakes
Marshes   Salt
                 pan   Ice cap
Sand desert limits   National Parks,etc.

© Oxford University Press

6

U.S.A. and Central America

Scale 1:19 000 000

0   200   400   600 km

Boundaries	International	(in sea)	(disputed)
	Internal		
Highways			
Railways			
Airports	International ⊕	Domestic ○	
Canals		Seasonal rivers, lakes	
Marshes		Salt pans	Ice cap
Sand desert limits		National Parks, etc.	

The United States

Alabama 23, Arizona 44, Arkansas 30, California 48, Colorado 40, Connecticut 6, Delaware 10,
Florida 17, Georgia 16, Idaho 42, Illinois 28, Indiana 20, Iowa 27, Kansas 35, Kentucky 21,
Louisiana 31, Maine 1, Maryland 11, Massachusetts 4, Michigan 18, Minnesota 26,
Mississippi 24, Missouri 29, Montana 38, Nebraska 34, Nevada 47, New Hampshire 2,
New Jersey 8, New Mexico 41, New York 7, North Carolina 14, North Dakota 32,
Ohio 19, Oklahoma 36, Oregon 46, Pennsylvania 9, Rhode Island 5, South Carolina 15,
South Dakota 33, Tennessee 22, Texas 37, Utah 43, Vermont 3, Virginia 13,
Washington 45, West Virginia 12, Wisconsin 25, Wyoming 39.
Alaska became a state on January 3, 1959 and Hawaii on August 21, 1959

Zenithal Equidistant Projection

© Oxford University Press

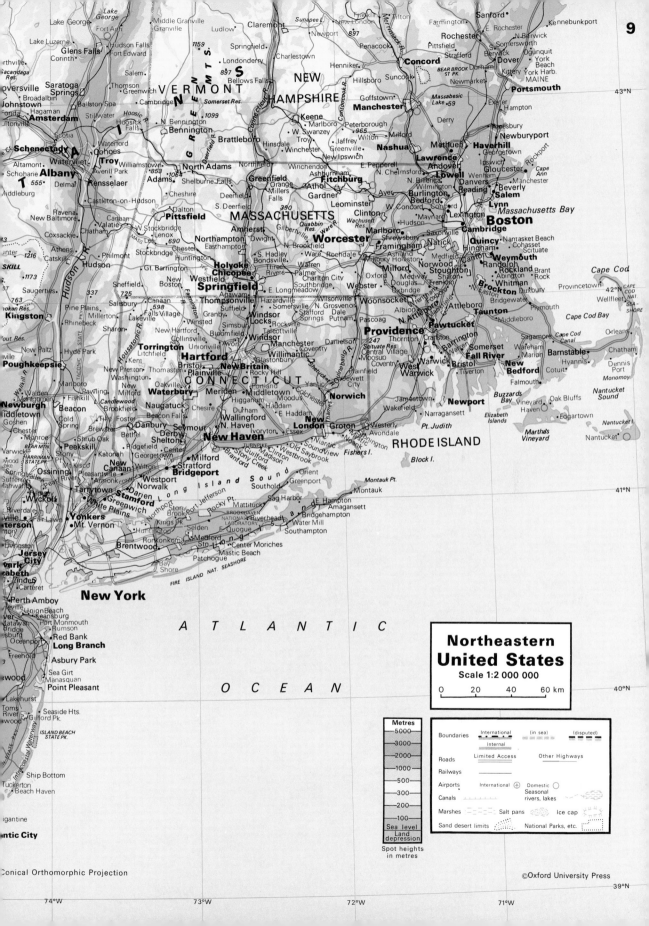

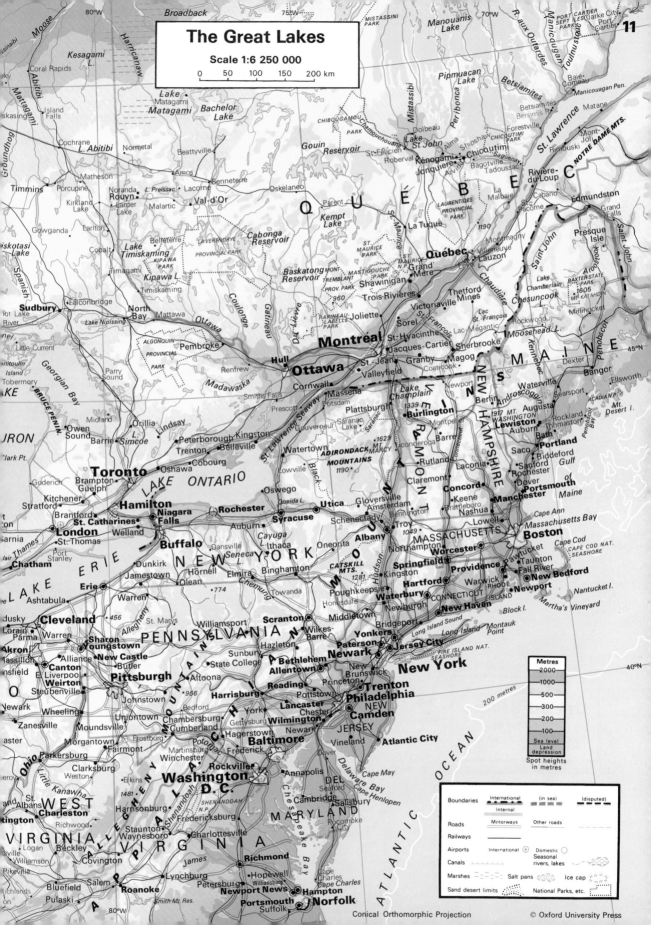

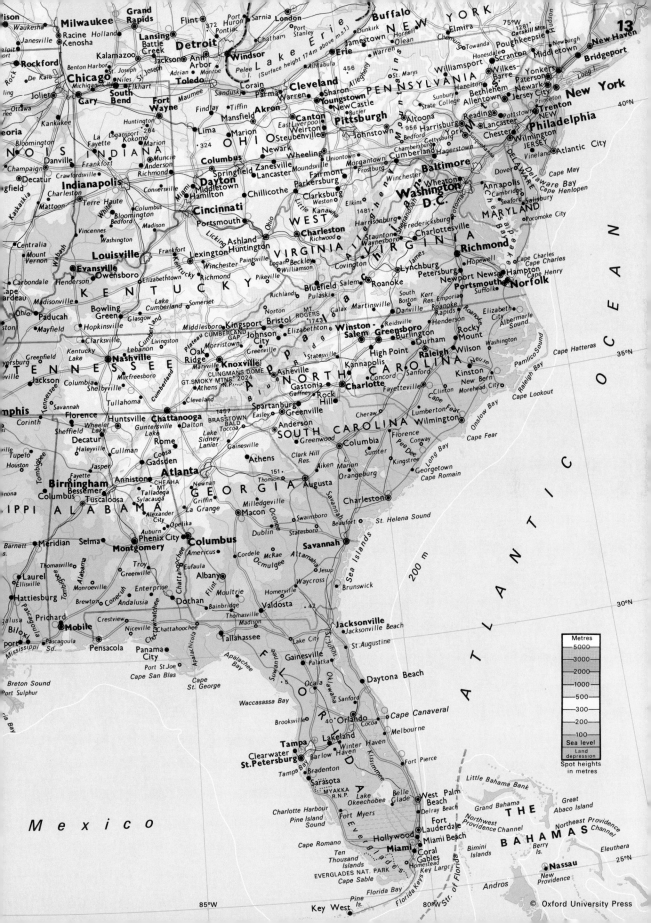

Pacific Coast: Canada & U.S.A.

Scale 1:6 250 000

0 50 100 150 200 km
0   100   200 km

Boundaries
International
Internal
(in sea)
(disputed)

Roads
Limited Access
International
Other Highways

Railways

Airports
International
Domestic

Canals

Marshes · Salt pans
Seasonal rivers, lakes
Ice cap

Sand desert limits
National Parks, etc.

© Oxford University Press

15.

Chihuahua
Cuauhtémoc
Delicias
Piedras Negras
Eagle Pass
Crystal City
Frio
Beeville
Conchos
TEXAS
Ciudad Camargo
BOLSÓN DE MAPIMÍ
Nueva Rosita
Melchor Múzquiz
Sabinas
Corpus Christi
Rio Grande
Bravo del Norte
Alice
Robstown
Kingsville
CHIHUAHUA
P.N. BARRANCA DEL COBRE
San Francisco del Oro
Hidalgo del Parral
Santa Bárbara
Jiménez
COAHUILA
Cuatrociénegas
Monclova
Presa de Don Martín
Salado
N U E V O
Sabinas Hidalgo
Laredo
Nuevo Laredo
UNITED STATES
Falcon Reservoir
Raymondville
CERRO MOHINORA 3992
CERRO CHORRERAS 3150
La Zarca
Zaragoza
2560
Presa de El Azúcar
Monterrey
Guadalupe
Edinburg
Mission
McAllen
Reinosa
Weslaco
Brownsville
Harli
Ben
Matan
Presa M. Hidalgo
Presa El Palmito
Gómez Palacio
San Pedro de las Colonias
General Cepeda
P.N. CUMBRES DE MONTERREY
Saltillo
L E Ó N
San Fernando
Sinaloa
Culiacán
Tepehuanes
El Palmito
Ciudad Lerdo
Torreón
Matamoros
Parras de la Fuente
Nazos
3050
Linares
Bahía de Santa María
Altata
San Lorenzo
Culiacán
DURANGO
L. de Santiaguillo
CERRO PEÑA NEVADA 4056
Ciudad Victoria
Ensenada del Pabellón
Eldorado
Piaxtla
CERRO PRIETO 3100
Matehuala
TAMAULIPAS
SIERRA DE TAMAULIPAS
Tropic of Cancer
3150 CERRO HUEHUETO
Durango
ZACATECAS
SAN
Ciudad Mante
Mazatlán
Rosario
Fresnillo de González Echeverría 2887
L U I S
Ciudad Madero
Tampi
L. del Caimanero
Zacatecas
3344 AHUALULCO
San Luis Potosí
P.N. EL GOGORRON
Cárdenas
Rio Verde
Ciudad de Valles
Pánuco
I. Palmito del Verde
Jerez de García Salinas
M E X I C O
P O T O S Í
Tuxpan
MEXICO
Tecuala
AGUAS-CALIENTES
2985
Las Tres Marías
Santiago Ixcuintla
NAYARIT
Aguascalientes
Teocaltiche
GUANAJUATO
S. Miguel de Allende
Querétaro
Ciudad de Dolores Hidalgo
Guanajuato
QUERÉTARO
HIDALGO
Mineral del Monte
Poza Rica
Papant
de Olart
Huauchinan
de la
Tuxpan
Id
Tepic
Lagos de Moreno
Ciudad del Morelos
León
Tepatitlán
San Francisco del Rincón
Silao
Irapuato
Salamanca
Celaya
Salvatierra
Acámbaro
San Juan del Rio
Pachuca de Soto
Tulancingo
Punta de Mita
Bahía de Banderos
Puerto Vallarta
Ameca
Tala
Guadalajara
Tlaquepaque
Ocotlán
Valle de Santiago
La Piedad
Moroleón
P.N. BOSENCHEVE
Teotihuacán
Tlalnepantla
TLAXCALA
PACIFIC
JALISCO
Cocula
L. de Chapala
La Barca
Sahuayo de Díaz
Zamora de Hidalgo
Jacona
L. de Cuitzeo
Ciudad Hidalgo
Morelia
Ciudad de México
Toluca
MEXICO
Tlalpan
Xochimilco
Cholula
Puebla
Atlixco
Oriz
Ciud
Medo
Autlán de Navarro
Sayula
Jiquilpan
Ciudad Guzmán
3749
Tamazula de Gordiano
Pátzcuaro
Zitácuaro
Heroica
Tenancingo de Degollado
Cuernavaca
POPOCATEPETL 5452
IXTACIHUATL
Tehua
3139
4339
P.N. VOLCAN DE COLIMA
Colima
PARICUTIN
2808
Uruapan del Progreso
DE TOLUCA
P.N. NEVADO
Zacatepec
Cuautla
MORELOS
Izúcar de Matamoros
PUEBL
Manzanillo
COLIMA
P.N. PICO DE TANCITARO
Apatzingán de la Constitución
MICHOACÁN
Taxco de Alarcón
Iguala de la Independencia
Jojutla de Juárez
Tecoman
2764
L. Infiernillo
289
Balsas
Melchor Ocampo
G U E R R E R O
Sierra
Atoyac
Madre
Huaj
de L
Bahía de Petacalco
Zihuatanejo
3703
Chilpancingo de los Braves
Tlapa de Comonfort 2840
Acapulco de Juárez
O C E A N
Puerto Escor

Mexico and Cuba

Scale 1:6 250 000

0   100   200 km

Conical Orthomorphic Projection
©Oxford University Press

Metres
5000
3000
2000
1000
500
300
200
100
Sea Level
Land Depression
Spot heights in metres

Boundaries	International	(in sea)	(disputed)
	Internal		
Roads	Limited access	Other highways	Tracks
Railways			
Airports	International ⊕	Domestic ○	
Canals		Seasonal rivers, lakes	
Marshes	Salt pans	Ice cap	
Sand desert limits	National Parks, etc.		

Tropic of Cancer

20°N

15°N

105°W   100°W

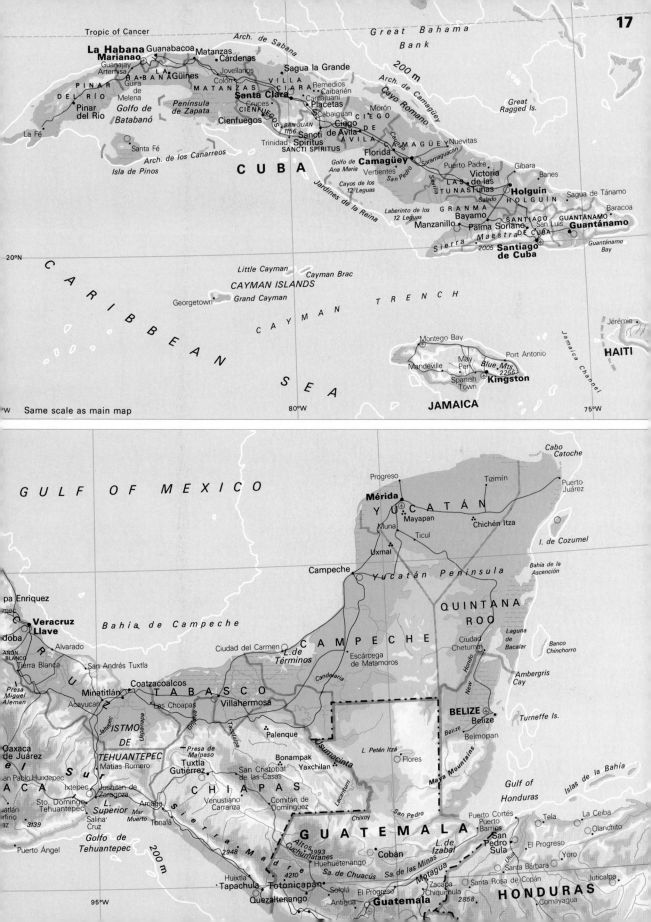

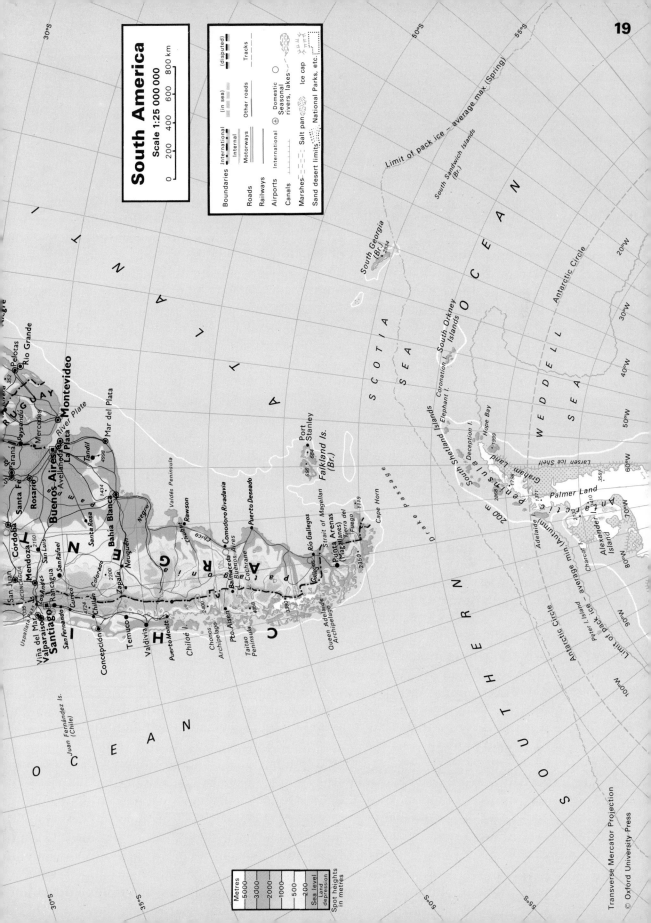

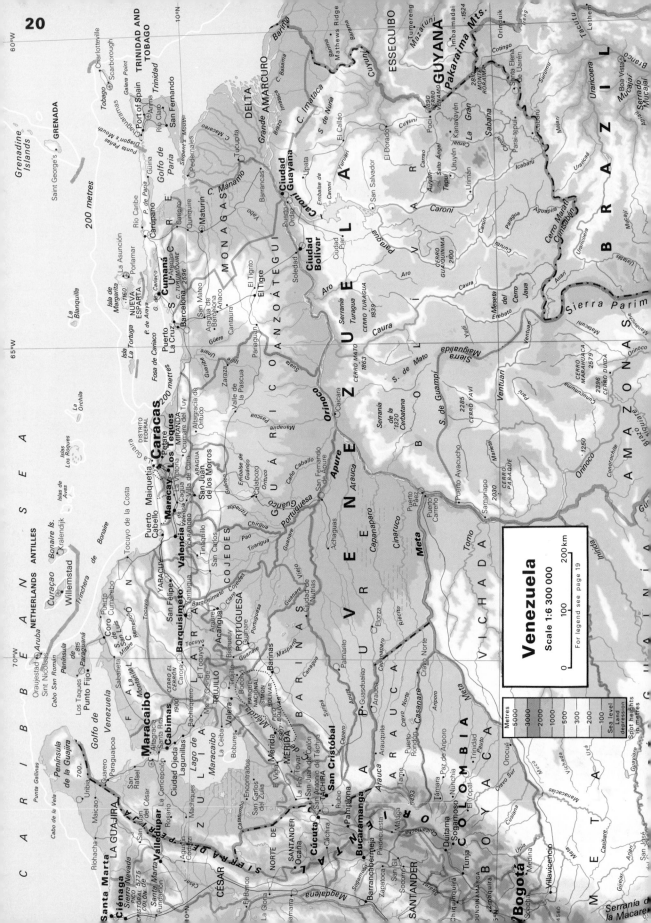

Venezuela

Scale 1:6 300 000

For legend see page 19

Metres	
5000	
3000	
2000	
1000	
500	
300	
200	
100	
Sea level	
Land depression	

Spot heights in metres

0   100   200km

Central South America

Scale 1:7 875 000

For legend see page 19

0   100   200 km

Atlantic Ocean

22

Scale 1:63 000 000

0 km 500   1000   1500   2000

Ocean Currents → Warm currents
-- -- Cold currents

Metres
5000
3000
2000
1000
500
300
200
100
Sea level
Land depression
200
3000
4000
5000
6000
Spot heights in metres

Modified Zenithal Equidistant Projection

© Oxford University Press

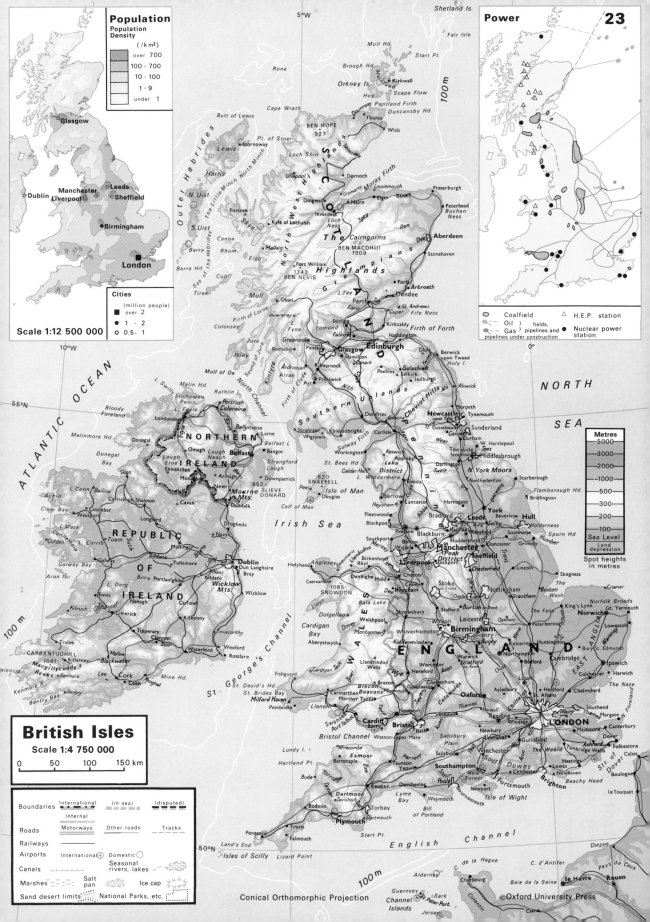

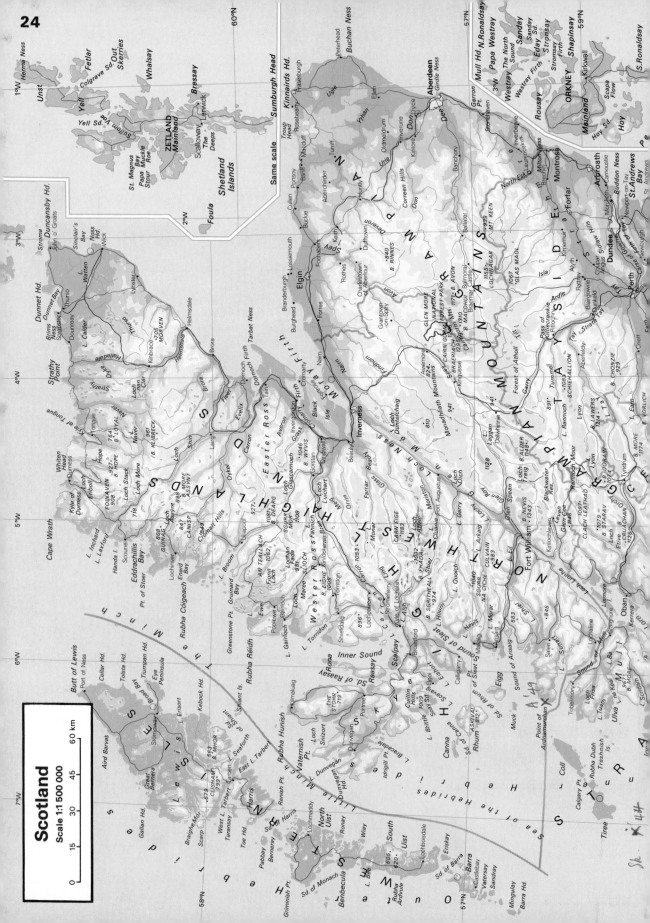

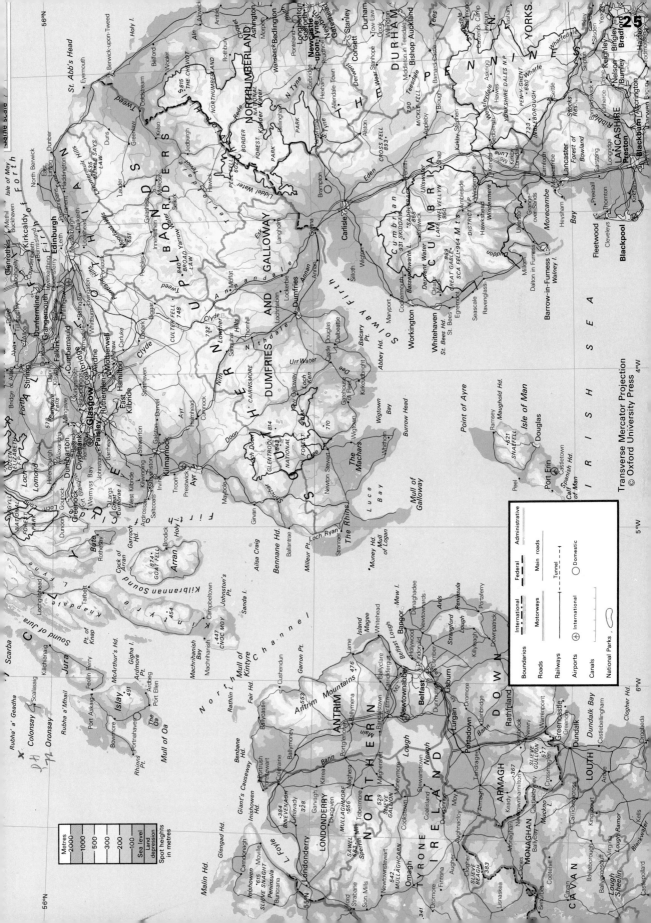

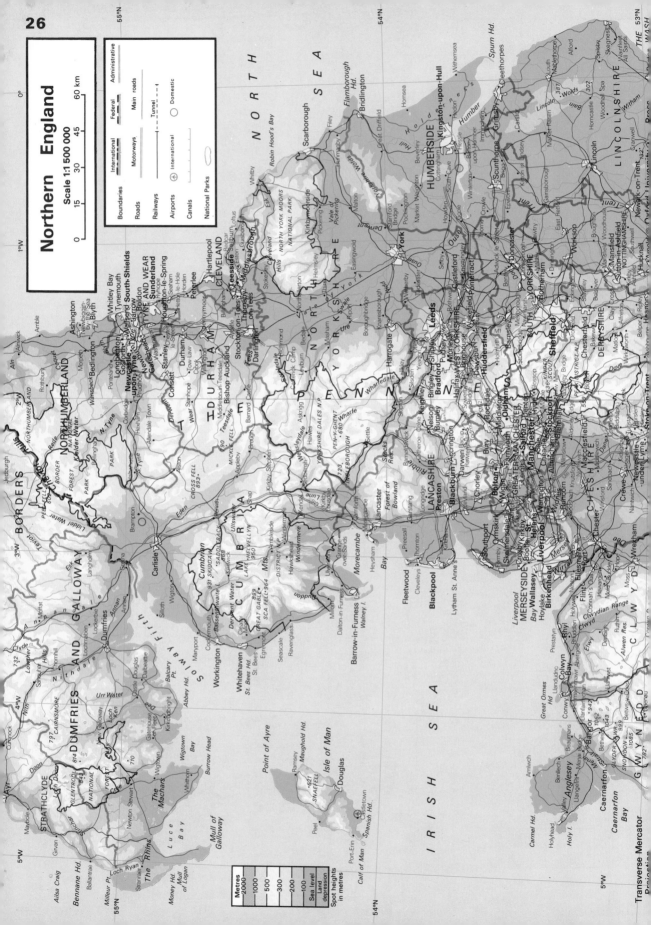

Southern England and Wales

Scale 1:1 500 000

0   15   30   45   60 km

Transverse Mercator Projection

© Oxford University Press

29

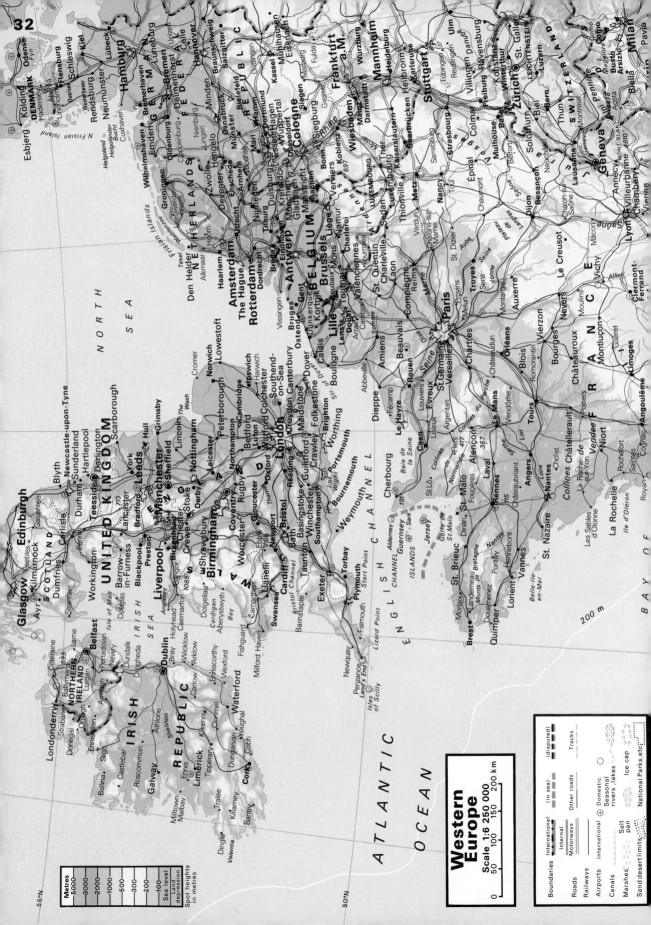

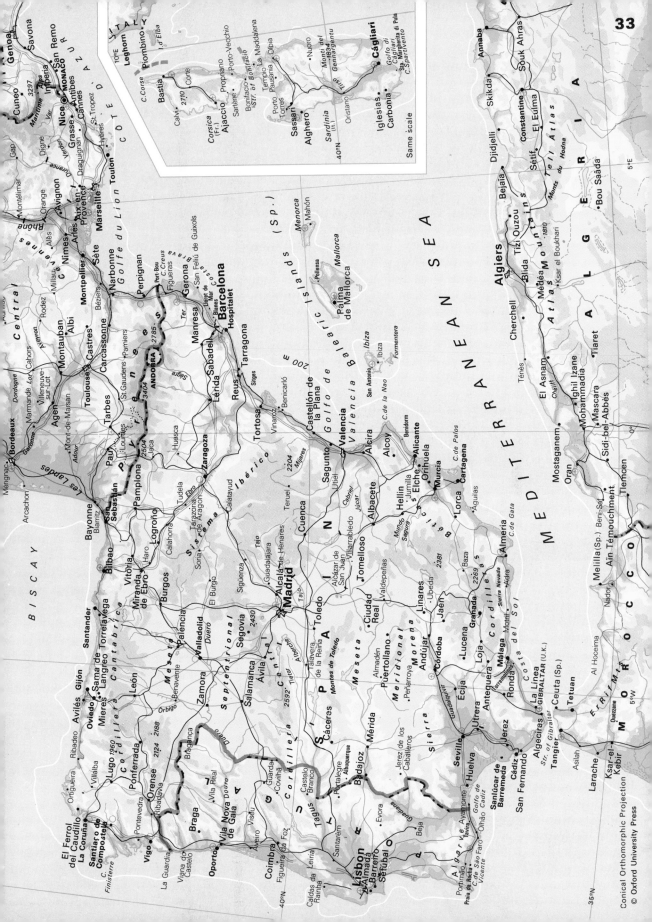

Eastern Europe

Scale 1:6 250 000

Conical Orthomorphic Projection

© Oxford University Press

Boundaries	International		
	Internal		(in sea)	(disputed)
Roads	Motorways		Other roads	Tracks
Railways			
Canals	International		
Airports		Domestic	
		Seasonal rivers, lakes	ice cap
	Salt pan	
	Marshes	
	Sand desert limits		National Parks, etc.

Metres
5000
3000
2000
1000
500
300
200
Sea Level
Land depression

Spot heights in metres

km 0 50 100 150 200 km

BLACK SEA

MARMARA

AEGEAN SEA

Sea of Crete

IONIAN SEA

ADRIATIC SEA

TYRRHENIAN SEA

MEDITERRANEAN SEA

ROMANIA — Bucharest, Ploiești, Constanța, Craiova, Pitești, Tirgu-Jiu

BULGARIA — Sofiya, Plovdiv, Varna, Burgas, Ruse, Stara Zagora

YUGOSLAVIA — Belgrade, Novi Sad, Sarajevo, Skopje, Niš, Titograd

ALBANIA — Tiranë, Durrës, Vlorë, Shkodër, Berat

GREECE — Athens, Thessalonica, Piraeus, Pátrai, Lárisa, Vólos

TURKEY — Istanbul, Edirne, Tekirdağ, İzmir, Balıkesir

ITALY — Rome, Naples, Palermo, Catania, Bari, Taranto

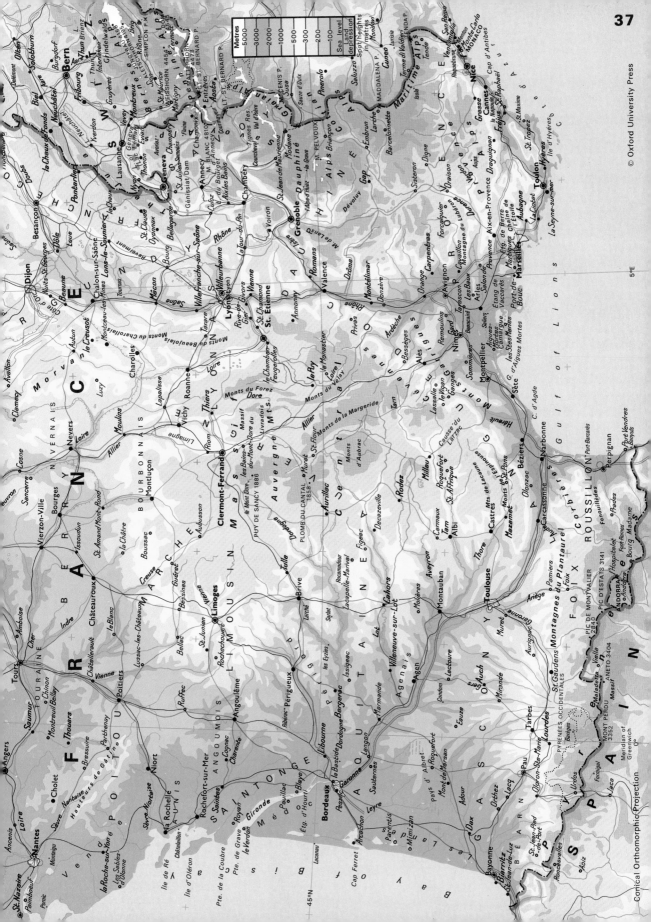

© Oxford University Press

Conical Orthomorphic Projection

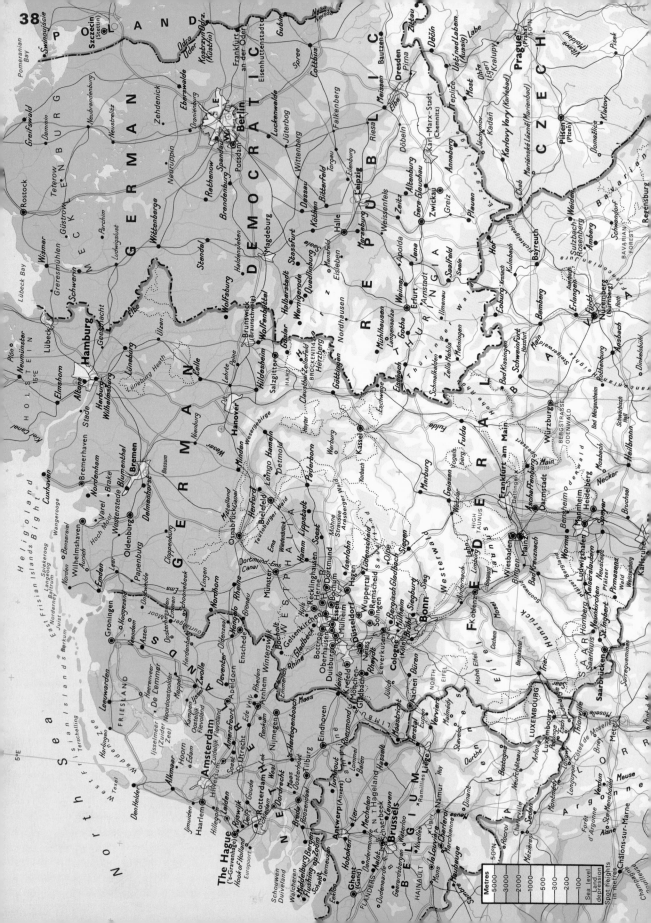

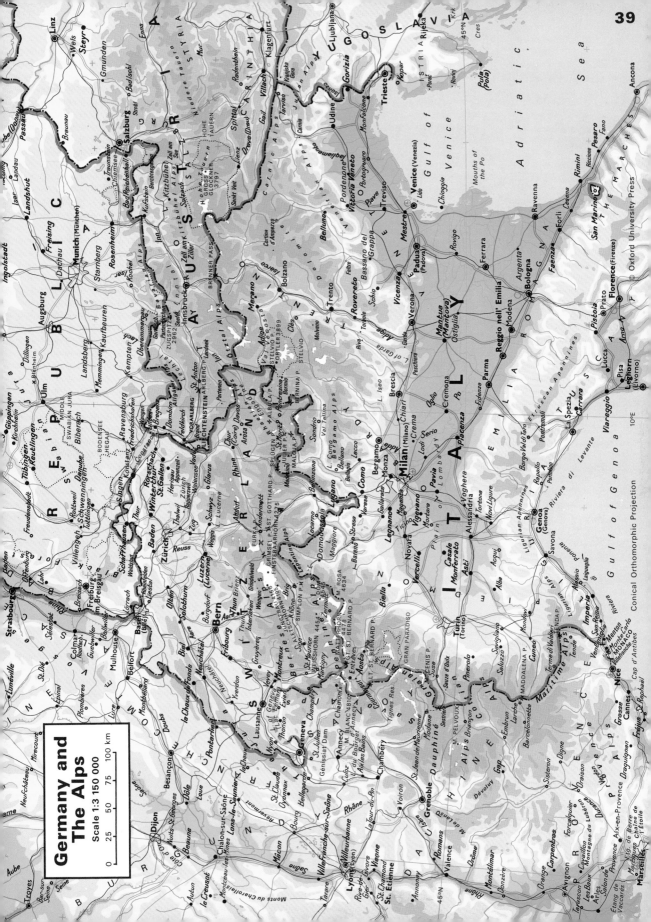

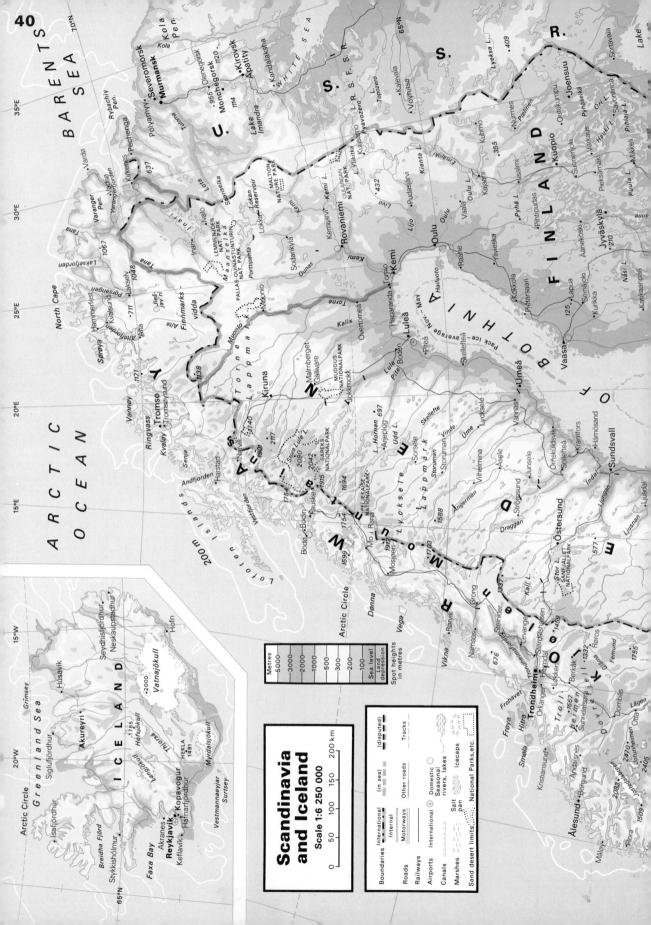

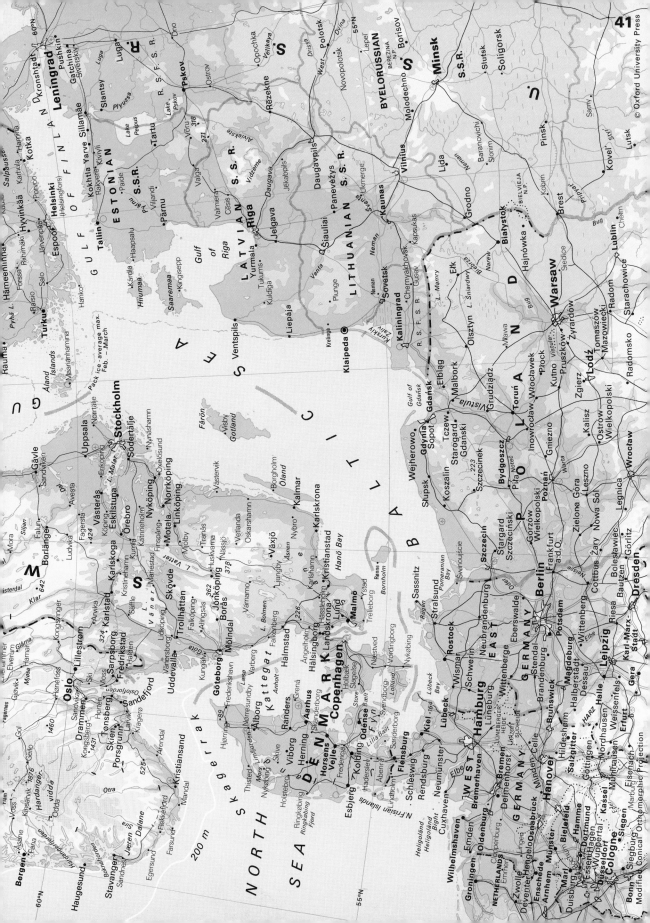
© Oxford University Press

North Pole

Metres
5000
3000
2000
1000
500
300
200
100
Sea level
Land depression

Spot heights in metres

Boundaries — International (in sea) (disputed)
Internal
Roads Motorways Other roads Tracks
Railways
Airports International ⊕ Domestic ○
Canals
Marshes Salt Pan
Seasonal rivers, lakes
Sand desert limits National Parks etc.
Ice cap

A L A S K A

I C E   O C E A N

Wiese I. (Vize)

Bol'shevik I.

Severnaya Zemlya

C. Chelyuskin

Taymyr Penin.

L. Taymyr

Nordvik

Khatanga
•601

Putoran Mts.
•1500

Norilsk
Dudinka
•1044

Igarka

Tarko-Sale

Gyda Penin.

G. of Yenisey
•402
•202

Kraul

F E D E R A T E D   S O C I A L I S T   R E P U B L I C

S.   S.   R.

Central Siberian Plateau

Plain

Lower Tunguska
•92

Stony Tunguska
•920

•623

Yeniseysk

Ob'

Chuna

Ust'-Kut

Angara

Tomsk
Kemerovo

Novosibirsk

Prokopyevsk
•2178

Barnaul

Biysk

Abakan Minusinsk
•2216
Novokuznetsk
•2248
Shalym

Kyzyl
•3019

Leninogorsk
•3254

Semipalatinsk

•2530

Lake Zaysan

NJIANG

•5500

Urumqi
•3962

Tulufan depression

Hami (Qomul)
•4252

•2800

ZIZHIQU

U I G H U R

•2809

Aerjinshanmai

Chaidamupendi

R E G I O N I

85°E 90°E 95°E

Laptev Sea

Tiksi

Kazachye
•1040

Novosibirskiye Ostrova
320

Lyakhov Islands
232
Laptev Str.
428

Verkhoyansk
•601

Olenek

Anabar

Vilyuy

Yakutsk

Elgyay
•190

Olekminsk

Dzharba

Vitim

Korshunova

Lena

Vitim

Zhigalova

Bratsk
•1022
•1728

Cheremknovo

Usol'ye

Irkutsk

Lake Baykal

Ulan-Ude

Selenga

Ulan Gom
•4116

Hovd
•2325

Uliastay
•4030

Altai Range
•3791

M O N G O L I A

Ulan Bator
•2505

Bulagan

Selenga

Sayn Shanda
•2838

Gobi Desert
•3810

Baotou

Hohhot

Anxi

Ala Shan

Yinchuan

Lanzhou
•4194
•6346

Xining

Huanghe

C H I N A

East Siberian Sea

Ostrovnoye

Ambarchik
•1674

Kolyma Plain

Indigirka
•819

Kolyma

Yukagir Plateau

Chersk iy Range
•2406
•2498
•3114 Susuman
•1847

Okhotsk
•1739

Magadan

Sea of Okhotsk

Aldan

Buyaga
•2101

Alan
•2481

•2155

Komsomolsk-na-Amur
•524

Nikolayevsk

Aleksandrovsk-Sakhalinskiy
544

Sakhalin

Soviet Harbour

Khabarovsk
•1868

Birobidzhan

Blagoveshchensk

Zeya

Tynda

Chekunda

Bureya

Ussuri

Sikhote Alin Range
•1853

Ussuriysk

Vladivostok

Partizansk

Yuzhno Sakhalinsk
•2299

Tarpeniya Bay

Wakkanai

Sapporo
Muroran
Hakodate
Amori

J A P A N

Sea of Japan

Peking

Tianjin

Tangshan

Bohai

Yantai

Qingdao

Yellow Sea

Jinan

Shijiazhuang

Taiyuan

Anyang

Luoyang

Xuzhou

Nanjing

Seoul

SOUTH KOREA
•1914

Pyongyang

NORTH KOREA
•2505

Nampo

Pusan

Hiroshima

Shimonoseki
Kitakyushu
•1772

Nagasaki

East China Sea

Conical Orthomorphic Projection

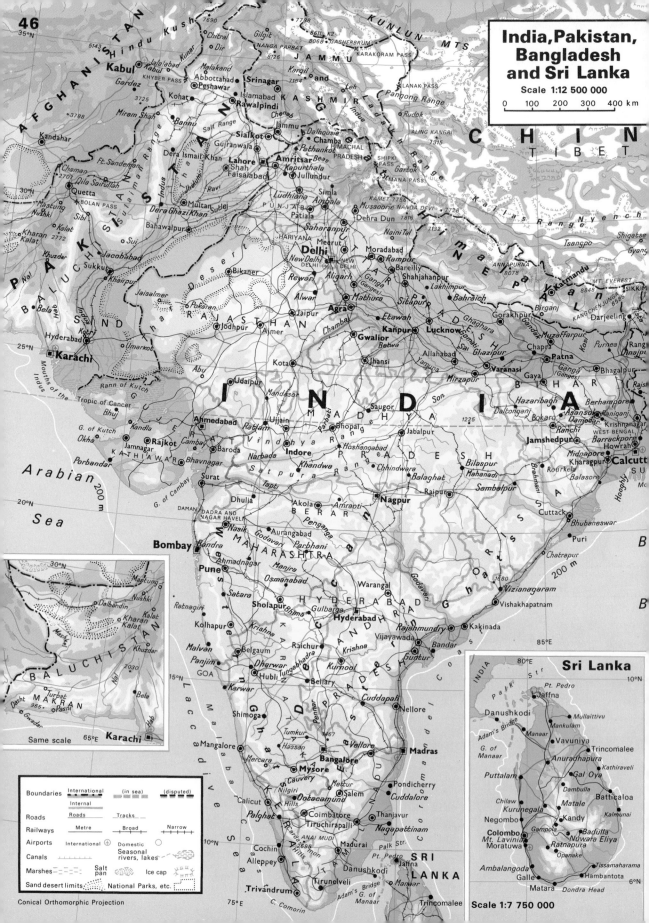

India, Pakistan, Bangladesh and Sri Lanka

Scale 1:12 500 000

0   100   200   300   400 km

Sri Lanka

Scale 1:7 750 000

Same scale

Conical Orthomorphic Projection

Boundaries — International   (in sea)   (disputed)
Internal
Roads — Roads   Tracks
Railways — Metre   Broad   Narrow
Airports — International ⊕   Domestic ○
Canals
Marshes   Salt pan   Ice cap
Sand desert limits   National Parks, etc.
Seasonal rivers, lakes

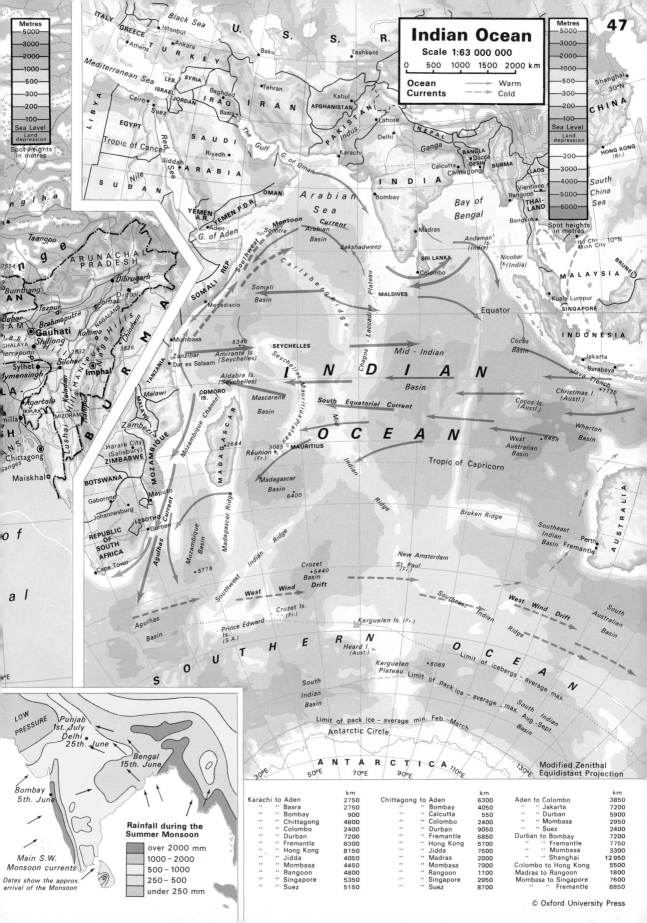

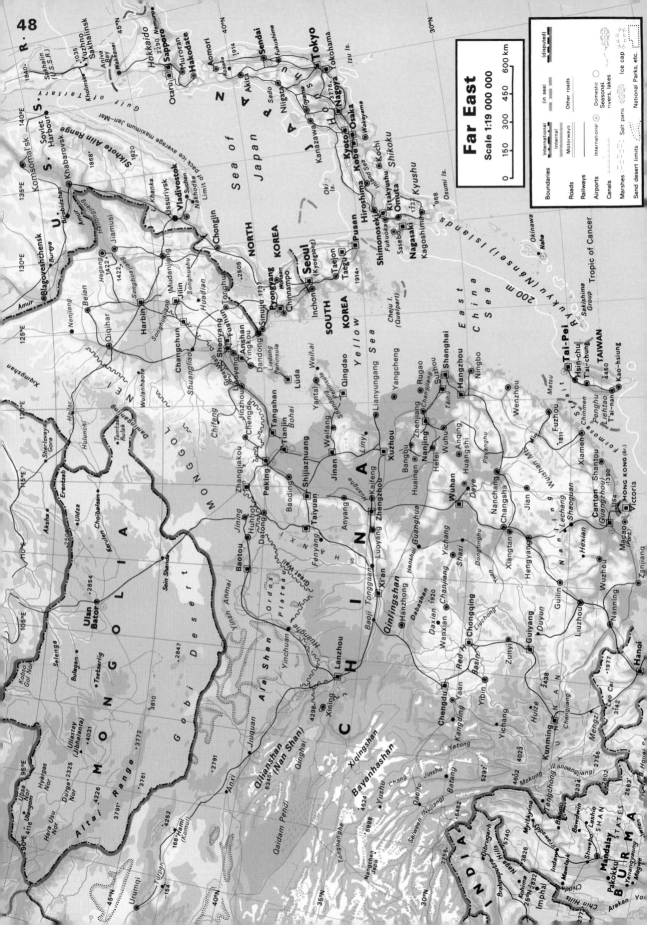

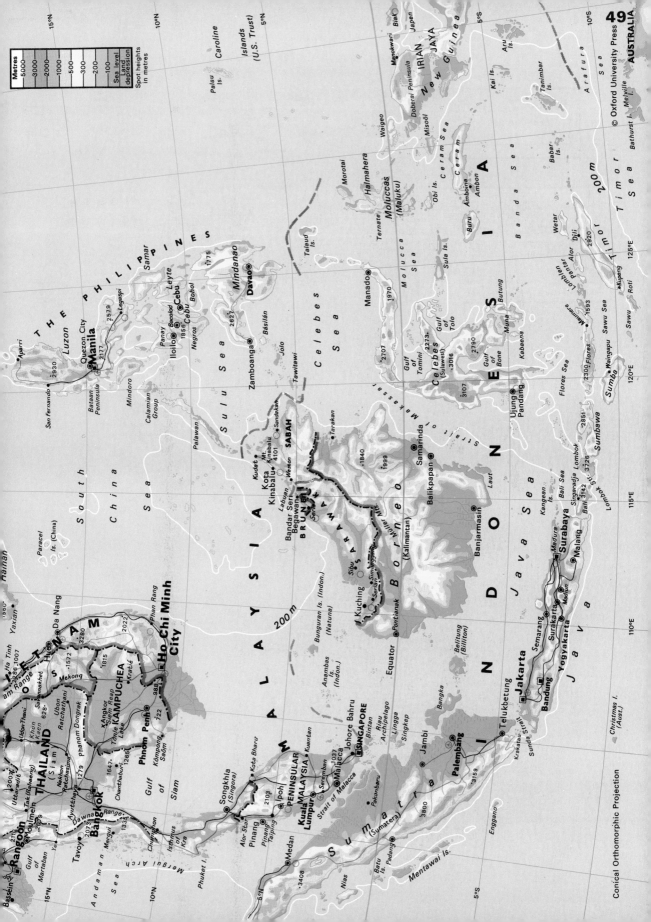

New Zealand

Scale 1:6 250 000

0   50   100   150   200 km

Boundaries — International — (in sea) — (disputed)
Roads — Motorways — Other roads — Tracks
Railways
Airports — International ⊕ — Domestic ○
Canals
Seasonal rivers, lakes
Marshes — Salt Pan — Ice cap
Sand desert limits — National Parks etc.

Three Kings Is.
C. Maria Van Diemen
North Cape
Kaitaia 751
Waitangi · Russell
Kaikohe 461
Whangarei
Hokianga Harbour
771
Dargaville
221
Great Barrier I.
Kaipara Harbour
Helensville
Hauraki Gulf
Devonport
Auckland
819
Papakura · Thames
Pukekohe · Paeroa
404 Huntly
95
Hamilton
Coromandel Ra.
Tauranga
Cambridge · Karapiro
Te Awamutu · Kawerau
962
Te Kuiti
808
Rotorua
Kinleith
Waikato
Volcanic Plateau
Waikarea
Taupo 1087
Murupara
822
Whakatane
Opotiki
Raukumara Ra.
1754
1213
L. Waikaremoana
UREWERA N.P.
Wairoa
Gisborne
Poverty Bay

NORTH ISLAND

BAY OF PLENTY

East Cape

New Plymouth · Waitara
TARANAKI
MT.EGMONT N.P.
2517 · Stratford
Opunake
Hawera
743
NGAURUHOE 2291
RUAPEHU 2797
TONGARIRO N.P.
Ohakune
Taumarunui
L. Taupo 1383
Kaimanawa Mts.
Ruahine Ra.
Taihape
Mahia Penin.
Hawke Bay
Napier
Hastings
Waipawa
Waigawa

Wanganui
Marton · Dannevirke
Feilding · Woodville
803
Palmerston North
C.Turnagain

C.Farewell
Golden Bay
Takaka
ABEL 1213
TASMAN N.P.
Tasman Mts.
Motueka
Tasman Bay
D'Urville I.
The Sounds
Nelson
1760 · Wairau
Blenheim
Tararua Ra.
1571
Masterton
Rimutaka Tunnel
663
Petone
536
Hutt
Wellington
Cook Strait
C.Palliser

MT.OWEN 1876
Westport
C.Foulwind
BULLER
Buller
NELSON LAKES N.P.
1501 · Reefton
Spenser Mts.
2338
MT TAPUAENUKU 2885
Kaikoura Ra.
965 · Kaikoura
Greymouth
Hokitika
ARTHURS PASS N.P.
Otira Tunnel
ARTHURS PASS
2400 · 1935
LEWIS P.
1875
Waiau
Hurunui
Waipara

SOUTH PACIFIC OCEAN

Tasman Sea

WESTLAND N.P.
MT TASMAN 3498
MT COOK 3764 N.P.
Hermitage
1951
MT ARROWSMITH 2795
2330
Riccarton
Pegasus Bay
Christchurch
Lyttelton
Akaroa
Banks Peninsula
Ashburton
Rakaia
Canterbury Plains
Canterbury Bight

Jackson Bay
Haast
MT. ASPIRING 2508
HAAST P. 3035
Southern Alps
1322
Timaru
Milford Sound
L. Wanaka
1871
Kurow
Oamaru
945

SOUTH ISLAND

FIORDLAND N.P.
1855
Queenstown
Cromwell
L. Wakatipu
1679
Alexandra
L. Te Anau
Kingston
Roxburgh
1449
Manapouri
1694
Lumsden
Edievale
1018
Doubtful Sound
1067
SOUTHLAND
Ohai
Gore
777
Port Chalmers
Otago Peninsula
Dunedin
Dusky Sound
C.Providence
Tuatapere
869
Clutha
720
Balclutha
Kaitangata
Invercargill
Bluff
Foveaux Strait
980
Stewart Island
Southwest Cape

200 m

Metres
5000
3000
2000
1000
500
300
200
100
Sea level
Land depression
Spot heights in metres

Conical Orthomorphic Projection

©Oxford University Press

Bounty Is. (N.Z.)

MALAYSIA

BRUNEI Bandar Seri Begawan

Kota Kinabalu   Sandakan   Tawitawi

SABAH   THE PHILIPPINES

Talaud Is.   Caroline Is.

Kota Bharu

5°N   PENINSULAR MALAYSIA

Kuantan

Natuna Is. (Indon.)

Anambas Is. (Indon.)

Malacca   Johore Bahru

SINGAPORE

Bintan   Lingga

0°

Kuching   Serian

•1840   SARAWAK

Sibu   Müller Mts.

Borneo

•1755   (Kalimantan)   •2278

Pontianak   Samarinda

Balikpapan

•189

Jambi

Bangka   Belitung (Billiton)

•3800   **Palembang**

3159   2232

Jakarta

Enggano   Sunda Str.

Bandung   Yogyakarta   Semarang •1602   **Surabaya**

Madura   Madiun   Malang •3265   •3676

Java   •3332

5°S

Lingga

Banjarmasin

Ujung Pandang

Laut   Strait of Makassar

Celebes Sea

Manado

Ternate

Molucca Sea

•2707   •1970

•2279   •3016.   Gulf of Tolo

•3019

•2239

•5030   Nassau Mts.

IRIAN   JAYA

Doberai Peninsula   •2940   Biak   Japen   New

Manokwari

Misoöl   Obi Is.   Seram   C. Vals

Buru   Ambon   •1731   Dolak I.

Banda Sea

Kai Is.   Aru Is.

I N D O N E S I A

Java Sea

Kangean Is.

Bali Sea   •3726   •2851   Sumbawa   •2300   Sawu Sea   Wetar   Lomblen   Alor   Dili   •2920

3142   2351   Flores Sea   Flores   Pantar

Sumba   •999   Waingapu   Kupang

Roti   Timor

Sawu

J a v a   Bali Str.   Lombok Str. Lombok

Christmas I. (Austl.)

I N D I A N

O C E A N

200 m

Melville

Bathurst   Darwin   Rum Jungle

Arnhem Land   Katherine

C. Talbot   Joseph Bonaparte Gulf   Daly   Birdum

Wyndham   Victoria   Daly Waters

Ord   Stuart   NORTHERN

Yampi Sound   C. Leveque   Dampier Land   Halls Creek •711   Tennant Creek   Barkly Tableland

Broome   Fitzroy   TERRITORY

80 Mile Beach   Great

Port Hedland   Mount Goldsworthy   Sandy Desert   L. Mackay

Monte Bello Is.   Marble Bar   Alice Springs

Dampier   Fortescue   Lake Disappointment   Macdonnell Ranges •1515

Exmouth Gulf   Hamersley Ra. •1226   Gibson Desert   Simpson Desert

Ashburton   Mt. Whaleback   WESTERN   •707

•342   •994   Oodnadatta

Carnarvon   **A U S T R A L I A**

Murchison   Meekatharra •564   Wiluna   Great Victoria Desert   SOUTH   Lake

Dirk Hartog I.   •594   AUSTRALIA   Mt. Eba   Leigh Cr.

Mt. Magnet   Laverton •565   •585

Geraldton   Leonora   Nullarbor Plain   Ooldea   Ceduna   Gairdner   Iron Knob   Whya   Port Augus

Coolgardie   Kalgoorlie   Zanthus   Forrest   Eucla   Port   Port Lincoln   Spencer

Northam   Southern Cross   Great   C. Catastrophe   Kang

Perth   Wagin   Esperance   Recherche   **Australian Bight**

Fremantle   Bunbury   •1109   Albany   Arch.

C. Naturaliste   C. Leeuwin

I R A

Arafura Sea

Timor Sea

Groote Eylandt   Gulf   Carper

Wel

Cam

Australasia

Scale 1:22 000 000

0 — 350 — 700 km

© Oxford University Press

Zenithal Equidistant Projection

Boundaries   International   (in sea)   (disputed)

Internal

Roads

Railways

Airports   International ⊕   Domestic ○

Canals   Seasonal rivers, lakes

Marshes   Salt pans   Ice cap

Sand desert limits   National Parks, etc.

Metres

5000

3000

2000

1000

500

300

200

100

Sea level

Land depression

Spot heights in metres

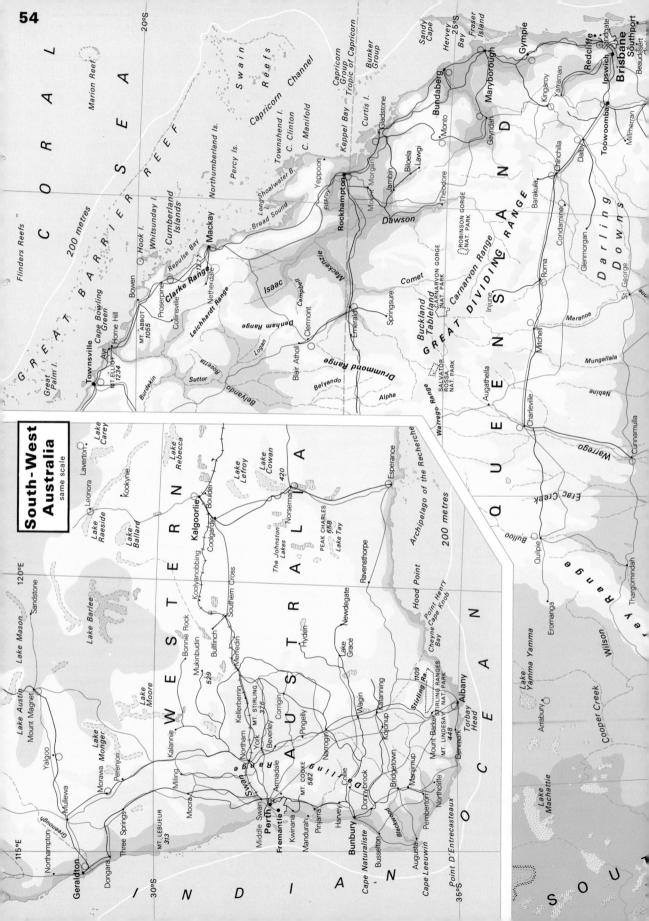

54

South-West Australia
same scale

GREAT BARRIER REEF

C O R A L   S E A

Flinders Reefs

Marion Reef

200 metres

Swain   Reefs

Capricorn   Channel

Capricorn Group

Tropic of Capricorn

Bunker Group

Sandy Cape

Hervey Bay

Fraser Island

25°S

Gympie

Kingaroy
Yarraman

Redcliffe
Sandgate
Ipswich **Brisbane**
Southport
Beaudesert

20°S

Northumberland Is.

Percy Is.

Townshend I.
C. Clinton
C. Manifold

Keppel Bay
Keppel I.

Curtis I.
Gladstone

Bundaberg
Monto

Gayndah

Maryborough

Millmerran
Toowoomba
Dalby
Chinchilla

Cumberland Islands

Hook I.
Whitsunday I.
Repulse Bay

Long Shoalwater B.
Broad Sound

Yeppoon
Rockhampton
Fitzroy

Mount Morgan

Jambin
Biloela
Lawgi

Theodore

Barakula
Condamine

Glenmorgan

St George

Mackay
Bowen
Proserpine
Collinsville Netherdale
Clarke Range 121.1

Leichhardt Range

Denham Range

Isaac

Dawson

Comet

Springsure

Buckland Tableland

Robinson Gorge NAT. PARK

Carnarvon Gorge NAT. PARK

Carnarvon Range

Roma

Mitchell

Maranoa

Mungallala

Nebine

Cape Bowling Green
Home Hill

Townsville
Great Palm I.
Ayr
Burdekin

MT. ABBOT 1055

Rosetta

Campbell

Clermont

Emerald

GREAT DIVIDING RANGE

Injune

Augathella

Charleville

Warrego

Cunnamulla

MT. ELLIOT 1234

Suttor

Belyando

Blair Atholl

Drummond Range

Belyando

Logan

Alpha

Warrego Range

SALVATOR ROSA NAT. PARK

Q U E E N S L A N D

D a r l i n g   D o w n s

Erac Creek

Bulloo

Quilpie

Eromanga

Arrabury

Cooper Creek

Thargomindah

Lake Machattie

Lake Yamma Yamma

Wilson

S O U T H

115°E

120°E

30°S

Lake Mason

Lake Austin

Sandstone

Lake Carey

Laverton

Leonora

Kookynie

Lake Rebecca

Lake Raeside

Lake Ballard

Lake Barlee

Mount Magnet

Yalgoo

Morawa
Perenjori

Lake Monger

Lake Moore

Mullewa

Greenough

Northampton

Three Springs

Mling
Moora

Geraldton
Dongara

MT. LESUEUR 313

W E S T E R N

Kalgoorlie
Boulder
Coolgardie

Koolyanobbing

Southern Cross

Bonnie Rock
Mukinbudin

Kalannie

Bullfinch
529

Kellerberrin
Merredin

Lake Lefroy

Lake Cowan
420

The Johnston Lakes

PEAK CHARLES 658
Lake Tay

Norseman

Esperance

Archipelago of the Recherche

200 metres

Hood Point

Cape Arid

Point Henry
Cape Knob

Ravensthorpe

Newdegate

Lake Grace

Hyden

Corrigin

A U S T R A L I A

I N D I A N   O C E A N

Kalannie

MT. STIRLING 376

York
Northam
Beverley

Swan Range

Armadale

Perth
Middle Swan
Fremantle
Kwinana

Mandurah
Pinjarra

Wagin

Katanning

Kojonup

Narrogin

Pingelly

MT. COOKE 582

D a r l i n g   R a n g e

Collie
Harvey
Dwellingbrook

Darkan

STIRLING RANGES NAT. PARK
1109

Stirling Ra.

MT. LINDESAY 448

Mount Barker

Albany
Torbay Head

Cranbrook

Tambellup

Manjimup

Bridgetown

Pemberton

Denmark

Bunbury
Busselton

Cape Naturaliste

Dunsborough

Northcliffe

Augusta

Cape Leeuwin

Point D'Entrecasteaux

35°S

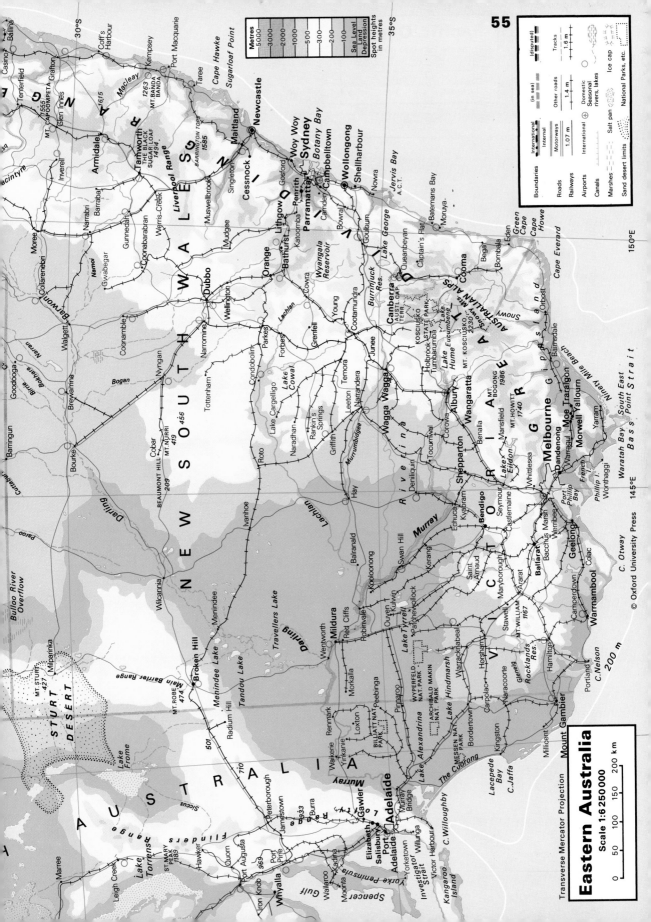

Boundaries · Roads · Railways · Airports · Canals · Marshes · Salt pan · Sand desert limits · National Parks, etc.

International · Internal (disputed) · Motorways · Other roads · Tracks · International · Domestic · Seasonal rivers, lakes · Ice cap

Metres · Sea Level · Land Depression · Spot heights in metres

Eastern Australia

Scale 1:6 250 000

Transverse Mercator Projection

0 50 100 150 200 km

© Oxford University Press

NEW SOUTH WALES

VICTORIA

STURT DESERT

MT. STURT 427
MILPARINKA

Marree
Leigh Creek
ST. MARY PEAK 1189
Lake Torrens
Lake Frome
Lake Eyre

Casino
Ballina
Tenterfield
Glen Innes
Coff's Harbour
Grafton
Armidale
Inverell
MT. CAPOOMPETA 1556
Macleay
Kempsey
Port Macquarie
Cape Hawke
Sugarloaf Point
Taree
MT. BANDA BANDA 1263
Barrington Tops 1585
Tamworth
THE BLACK SUGAR LOAF 1494
Liverpool Range
Singleton
Maitland
Newcastle
Woy Woy
Gosford
Sydney
Botany Bay
Wollongong
Shellharbour
Nowra
Jervis Bay
A.C.T.
Batemans Bay
Moruya
Bega
Bombala
Eden
Green Cape
Cape Howe
Cape Everard

Muswellbrook
Cessnock
Penrith
Parramatta
Campbelltown
Camden
Bowral
Goulburn
Lithgow
Katoomba
Bathurst
Orange
Mudgee
Wyangala Reservoir
Cowra
Young
Cootamundra
Queanbeyan
Canberra
AUSTL. CAP. TERR.
Captain's Flat
Lake George
Burrinjuck Res.
KOSCIUSKO STATE PARK
Tumbarumba
Holbrook
MT. KOSCIUSKO 2230
Lake Hume
Lake Eucumbene
Snowy
Cooma
AUSTRALIAN ALPS
MT. BOGONG 1986
Orbost

Tamworth
Barraba
Narrabri
Gunnedah
Coonabarabran
Werris Creek
Wellington
Dubbo
Parkes
Forbes
Grenfell
Temora
Junee
Wagga Wagga
Narrandera
Leeton
Griffith
Albury
Wangaratta
Benalla
Corowa
Tocumwal
MT. HOWITT 1740
Mansfield
MT. BUFFALO

Moree
Collarenebri
Walgett
Coonamble
Gilgandra
Narromine
Tottenham
Condobolin
Lake Cowal
Lake Cargelligo
Rankin's Springs
Naradhan
Hay
Deniliquin
Kyabram
Echuca
Shepparton
Seymour
Lake Eildon
Whittlesea
Melbourne
Dandenong
Port Phillip Bay
Phillip I.
French I.
Wonthaggi
Warragul
Moe
Traralgon
Morwell
Yallourn
Yarram
Gippsland
Bairnsdale
Lakes Entrance
Ninety Mile Beach
Waratah Bay
South East Point
Bass Strait

Goodooga
Barringun
Bourke
Brewarrina
Nyngan
Cobar
BEAUMONT HILL 456
MT. NJURI 419
Roto
Ivanhoe
Balranald
Swan Hill
Kerang
Bendigo
Castlemaine
Saint Arnaud
Maryborough
Stawell
Ararat
Ballarat
Bacchus Marsh
Geelong
Colac
Camperdown
Warrnambool
C. Otway
C. Nelson

Bulloo River Overflow
Paroo
Barringun
Wanaaring
Wilcannia
Menindee
Menindee Lake
Broken Hill
MT. ROBE 474
Tandou Lake
Travellers Lake
Darling
Wentworth
Mildura
Red Cliffs
Robinvale
Morkalla
Ouyen
Patchewollock
Lake Tyrrell
Kulwin
WYPERFELD NAT. PARK
ARCHIBALD MAKIN NAT. PARK
Warracknabeal
Horsham
Hamilton
Rocklands Res.
Glenelg
Portland
200 m

Darling
MT. NUMBER 501
Radium Hill
Broken Hill
Main Barrier Range
Peebinga
Pinnaroo
Renmark
Berri
Waikerie
Loxton
BILLIATT NAT. PARK
THE MESSENT NAT. PARK
Bordertown
Kingston
Naracoorte
Carpolac
Coleraine
Millicent
Mount Gambier

MT. ROBE
Peterborough
Jamestown
Burra
MT. 933
Gladstone
Port Pirie
Crystal Brook
Murray Bridge
Tailem Bend
Meningie
Lake Alexandrina
The Coorong
Lacepede Bay
C. Jaffa
Kingston

Whyalla
Iron Knob
Port Augusta
Quorn
Hawker
Wilmington
Port Germein
MT. 969
Gulf
Spencer Gulf
Gawler
Elizabeth
Salisbury
Adelaide
Port Adelaide
Willunga
Yorketown
Edithburgh
Victor Harbour
Yorke Peninsula
Investigator Strait
Kangaroo Island
C. Willoughby
Moonta
Wallaroo
Kadina
Maitland
Flinders Range
Lofty Range

Liverpool Range
Namoi
Bogan
Lachlan
Murrumbidgee
Murray
Lachlan
Darling
Riverina
Gwydir
Barwon
Macintyre
Castlereagh
Bellinger

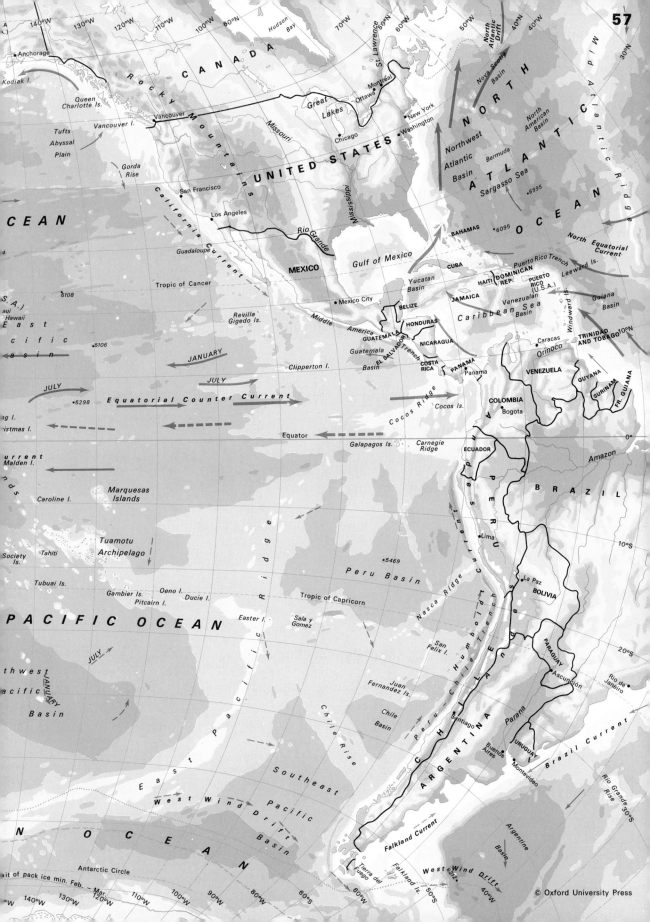

CANADA

UNITED STATES

MEXICO

Anchorage

Kodiak I.

Queen
Charlotte Is.

Tufts
Abyssal
Plain

Vancouver I.

Vancouver

Rocky Mountains

Great
Lakes

Missouri

Hudson
Bay

Ottawa

Montréal

New York

Washington

St. Lawrence

NORTH ATLANTIC OCEAN

North
Atlantic
Drift

Nova Scotia
Basin

Mid Atlantic Ridge

San Francisco

Los Angeles

California Current

Guadaloupe Current

Gorda
Rise

Tropic of Cancer

OCEAN

6108

Revilla
Gigedo Is.

Mexico City

Rio Grande

Gulf of Mexico

Northwest
Atlantic
Basin

Bermuda

Sargasso Sea

North
American
Basin

•6995

North Equatorial
Current

BAHAMAS

•6095

CUBA

Yucatan
Basin

HAITI

JAMAICA

DOMINICAN
REP.

PUERTO
RICO
(U.S.A.)

Puerto Rico Trench

Leeward Is.

Guiana
Basin

S. A.)

aui

Hawaii

East

Pacific

Basin

•5106

JANUARY

JULY

Middle
America

GUATEMALA

HONDURAS

NICARAGUA

Guatemala
Basin

EL SALVADOR

Trench

COSTA
RICA

PANAMA

BELIZE

Caribbean Sea

Venezuelan
Basin

Windward Is.

Caracas

Orinoco

TRINIDAD
AND TOBAGO

Guayana

Guiana
Basin

Clipperton I.

JULY

Equatorial Counter Current

•5298

ng I.

ristmas I.

Equator

Galapagos Is.

Cocos Ridge

Cocos Is.

Carnegie Ridge

COLOMBIA

Bogota

ECUADOR

Amazon

BRAZIL

Panama

VENEZUELA

GUYANA

SURINAM

FR. GUIANA

rrent

Malden I.

nds

Caroline I.

Marquesas
Islands

Tahiti

Society
Is.

Tubuai Is.

Tuamotu
Archipelago

Gambier Is.

Oeno I.

Ducie I.

Pitcairn I.

Easter I.

Sala y
Gomez

Lima

Peru Basin

•5469

Tropic of Capricorn

Nasca Ridge

La Paz

BOLIVIA

PARAGUAY

Asunción

Rio de
Janeiro

East Pacific Ridge

PACIFIC OCEAN

thwest

acific

Basin

JULY

JANUARY

San
Felix I.

Fernandez Is.

Juan
Fernandez Is.

Chile
Basin

Chile Rise

Southeast
Pacific
Basin

West Wind Drift

Santiago

Andes

Peru-Chile Trench

Humboldt Current

CHILE

ARGENTINA

URUGUAY

Montevideo

Buenos
Aires

Paraná

Brazil Current

Rio Grande Rise

Argentine
Basin

N

OCEAN

Antarctic Circle

it of pack ice min. Feb. - Mar.

Tierra del
Fuego

Falkland Current

Falkland Is.

West Wind Drift

140°W

130°W

120°W

110°W

100°W

90°W

80°W

70°W

60°W

50°W

40°W

30°W

30°S

20°S

10°S

0°

10°N

© Oxford University Press

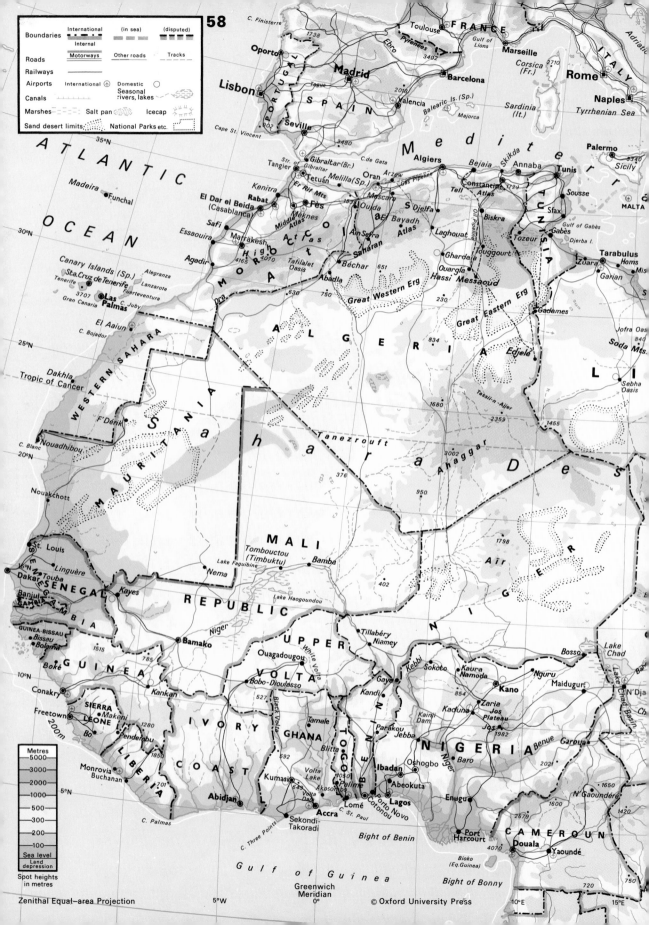

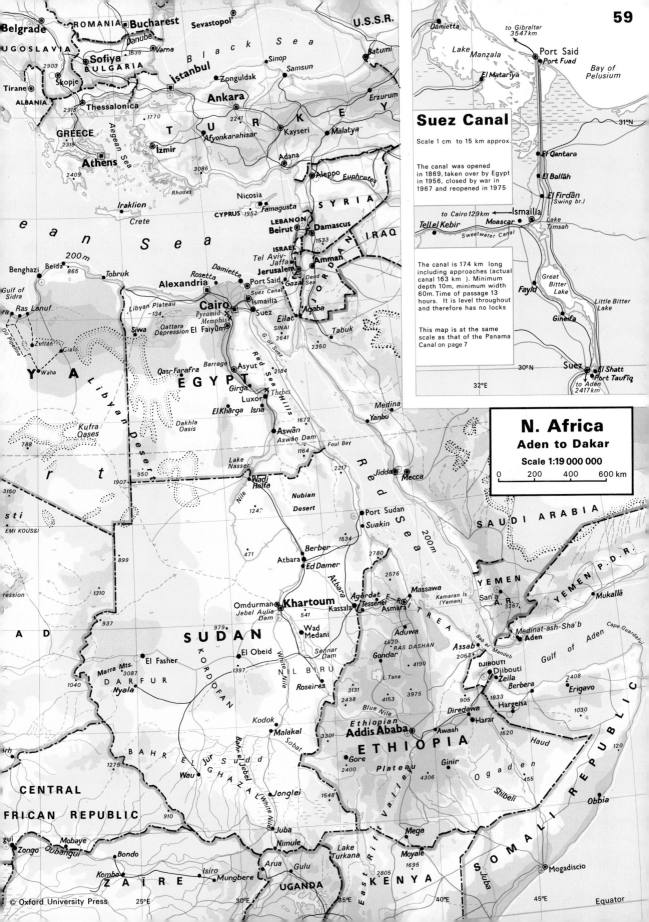

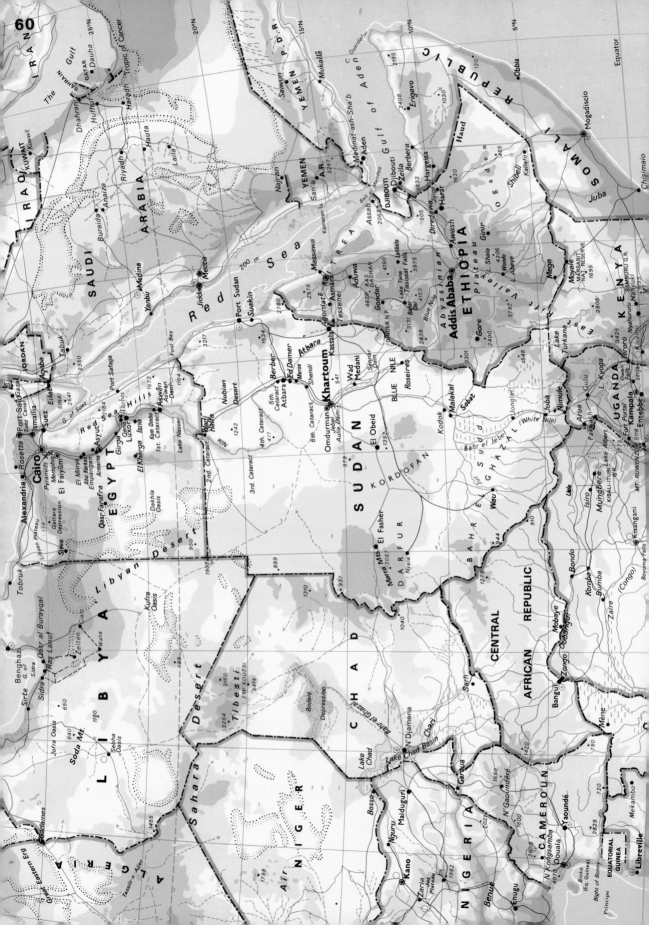

East and Southern Africa

Scale 1:19 000 000

0 200 400 600 km

61

© Oxford University Press

Zenithal Equal Area Projection

Boundaries
International
Internal

Roads
Motorways
International
Other roads

Railways
Airports International

Canals
Marshes
Sand desert limits

(in sea)
(disputed)

Tracks

Domestic
Seasonal rivers, lakes
Salt pans
Ice cap

National Parks etc...

Metres
5000
3000
1000
500
300
200
100
Sea Level
Land Depression

Spot heights in metres

INDIAN OCEAN

ATLANTIC OCEAN

MADAGASCAR

COMORO ISLANDS

Mozambique Channel

Toamasina
Antananarivo
Fianarantsoa
Antsiranana
Nossi Bé
Mahajanga
Morondava
Toliary
Faradofay
C. Sainte Marie
Bassas da India (Fr.)
Europa (Fr.)

Aldabra Is. (Seychelles)

TANZANIA
MALAWI
MOZAMBIQUE
ZAMBIA
ZIMBABWE
BOTSWANA
ANGOLA
NAMIBIA (S. W. AFRICA)
SOUTH AFRICA
REPUBLIC OF
BURUNDI
LESOTHO
SWAZILAND
CAPE PROVINCE
TRANSVAAL
ORANGE FREE STATE
NATAL
TRANSKEI

Malindi
Mombasa
Tanga
Zanzibar
ZANZIBAR
Dar es Salaam
Pemba
Mtwara
Mozambique
Pemba
Nachingwea
Nampula
Entre Rios
Quelimane
Mocuba
Songea
Lichinga
Zomba
Beira
Blantyre
Lilongwe
Salima
Harare City / Salisbury
Umtali
Que Que
Bulawayo
Messina
Maputo
Pietermaritzburg
Durban
East London
Port Elizabeth
Pretoria
Johannesburg
Mbabane
Ladysmith
Maseru
Bloemfontein
Kimberley
Mafikeng
Gaborone
Serowe
Francistown
Windhoek
Walvis Bay
Lüderitz
Swakopmund
Port Nolloth
Springbok
Beaufort West
Victoria West
De Aar
Worcester
Oudtshoorn
Cape Town
Cape of Good Hope
C. Agulhas

Mwanza
Dodoma
Tabora
Mpanda
Kigoma
Bujumbura
Bukavu
Kindu
Kongolo
Kamina
Kananga
Lusambo
Kapanga
Ilebo
Kasai
Luanda
Benguela
Lobito
Mocâmedes
Menongue
Huambo
Malanje
Quibala
Kinshasa
Brazzaville
Pointe Noire
Lobito
Mbala
Kasama
Ndola
Kitwe
Lubumbashi
Likasi
Mongu
Balovale
Lusaka
Kafue
Maramba
Wankie
Kasane
Tsumeb

Mt. Kilimanjaro 5895
Moshi

Lake Malawi
Lake Tanganyika
Lake Rukwa
Lake Mweru
Lake Bangweulu
Lake Kariba
Lake Ngami
Lualaba
Zambezi
Limpopo
Orange
Kalahari Desert
Namib Desert
Etosha Pan
Victoria Falls

Tropic of Capricorn

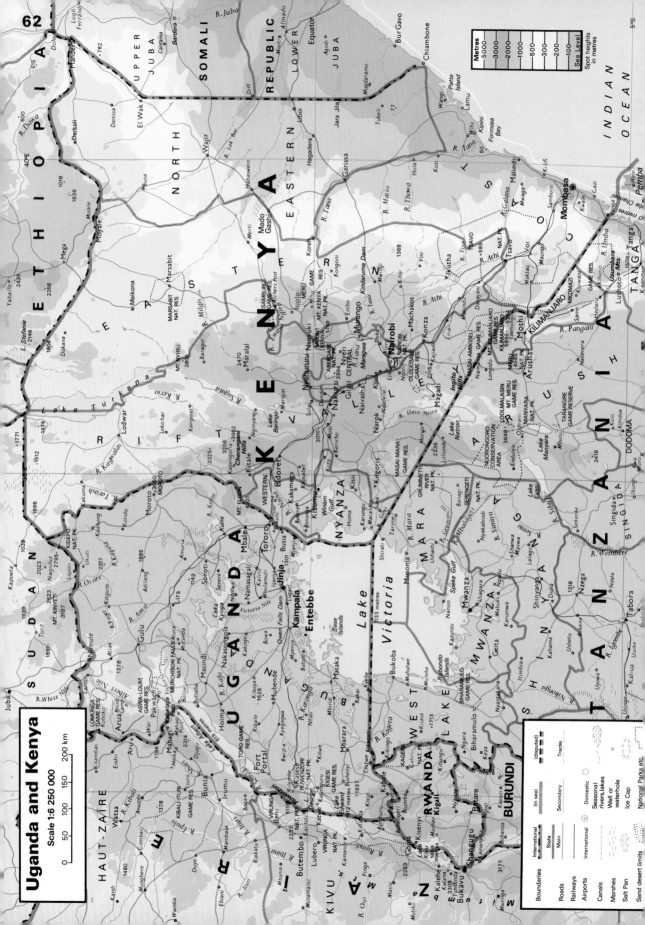